MIND OVER MONEY

Why Most People Lose
Money in the Stock
Market and How You Can
Become a Winner

by JEROME TUCCILLE

WILLIAM MORROW AND COMPANY, INC.
NEW YORK   1980

Copyright © 1980 by Jerome Tuccille

Library of Congress Cataloging in Publication Data

Tuccille, Jerome.
  Mind over money.

  1. Stocks—United States. 2. Investments—
Psychological aspects. I. Title.
HG4921.T82   332.6'322   79-22813
ISBN 0-688-03595-7

Book design by Bernard Schleifer

Printed in the United States of America

First Edition

1 2 3 4 5 6 7 8 9 10

TO *Marie,*
my first, second, third, and best wife

Contents

The brokerage firm mentioned in this book, Bull, Banks, Forbes & Trotsky, is a composite of the major investment firms on Wall Street and not a fictitious name for any particular firm. The same is true of Lenny, Gil, Dale, Paul, and other brokers and investors characterized in these pages. They are composites, drawn from real situations, rather than depictions of specific individuals. The stories and dialogue are presented strictly to dramatize my theories about people and their financial habits. Any similarity they might bear to living individuals is strictly coincidental.

JEROME TUCCILLE

PART ONE

WHY MOST PEOPLE LOSE MONEY IN THE STOCK MARKET

CHAPTER ONE

A Dangerous Notion

DON'T LOOK NOW, but a dangerous notion is afoot in the land. If we fail to exercise due diligence in face of it we run the risk of being overwhelmed by the same devastating force with which the bubonic plague swept Europe in the Middle Ages.

Through all of history mankind has been deluded by one lunatic belief or another. For a while the most reputable among us swore that the earth was flat. Those who entertained a contrary theory risked being clapped in chains or having their heads disengaged from the rest of their bodies. Not only was the earth flat, but it also reigned supreme at the center of the universe. It took a rather persistent and courageous gentleman named Copernicus to disabuse us of that notion.

At different stages in our historical development the human race has held equally strong (and equally wrong) views on a broad range of subjects. Not only were these views held by those in command, but our political and religious leaders through the ages have shown a fondness for inflicting pain and death on those who dared to disagree with them. And so our fellow citizens on Planet Earth have been willing to fight and die for all sorts of erroneous views—the belief in the divine right of kings and other political dictators, the notion that solar eclipses were warnings from the Deity, that epileptics were possessed by devils, that dragons lived in the forest, that war is good for the economy, and other fanciful delusions.

When it comes to gullibility, no one can accuse this human race of ours of taking second place to any other species. No wonder we are at the mercy of every quack and schemer, every crooner with a song to sing, every huckster with a bag of tricks who comes dancing down the pike. We have been fleeced and taken to the cleaners by all sorts of fast-talking romancers. That we have managed not only to survive, but to prosper and advance into these last decades of the twentieth century, is testimony to our ability to separate fact from fiction in the final analysis. We have stumbled close to the brink innumerable times, only to pull away at the last moment and find our way back to the civilized path. Flirting with doom, we have managed to escape each time with our necks still intact. It's enough to give one hope for the future. It's enough to make me an optimist.

"What has all this got to do with money?" you ask. A lot. Let me explain.

Money is a subject as much misunderstood today as eclipses were a millennium or so ago. Eclipses were magic, the multitudes used to say. Well, money is regarded by otherwise sane and normal people with the same bewilderment that eclipses were in past centuries. The dangerous notion I was referring to a moment ago is the one which holds that people understand what money is and use it to further their own best interests.

The point of this book is that this, quite simply, is not the case. Money is every bit as complicated as sex and the mania some of us have for controlling other people's lives, and money may well be the final Great Mystery of the Universe yet to be unraveled by science. The danger involved stems from the fact that money is the fuel which keeps the machinery of civilization operating. Without it we can do nothing. We cannot feed or shelter ourselves, provide for our offspring, maintain the health of the body or the peace of the human psyche.

Money is so closely tied in to human behavior and personal psychology that it has to share top billing with Sex and Power as one of the key reasons why people run off to have their ids massaged on the psychiatrist's couch. All of us are neurotic to one extent or another. The first sign of mental health is being able, finally, to acknowledge this fact about oneself and proceed accordingly. The only variables are the degree to which each of us is neurotic, and the precise nature of our personal anxieties. Once you've got the handle on these, you're three skips ahead of the rest of the world. The people I fear the most are the ones who claim they are normal and have all the answers—the Ayn Rands, Werner Ehrhards, and other cultists of the world. When I see them walking down my block I know enough to grab my wallet, lock the doors, and hide under my bed until the danger passes.

During the last decade or so we seem to have made some advances in solving the riddles of sex and power. Starting in the late sixties, every other book reaching the stores had to do with one aspect of sex or another: heterosex and homosex, marital and extramarital sex, open and closed sex, clitoral, vaginal, and anal sex, liberated and unliberated sex. The mind boggles, spins, and roars into orbit. The sex books were followed by the power books—how to get it and use it on others, how to keep others from using it on you, how to dress for power, eat, act, and sleep for power. If the *Kama Sutra* seems outdated by the sex manuals, Hitler's *Mein Kampf* pales against the backdrop of the power books. We won't go into the diet books here, but that's a whole different dimension in human neurosis. It has to do with compulsion, the compulsion for food to fill an inner need somewhat akin to the compulsion for alcohol and other drugs. No matter how you slice it, compulsion is neurotic.

The money books, on the other hand, talk about money as though we all understood what it was in the first place. They talk about systems, how to beat the odds in the stock and commodities markets; they talk about charts and fundamentals and other economic exotica. I've written a couple of these books myself, and they have their place for *those who know what they want from their money.*

But, in retrospect, this is one king-sized assumption to make. This is the dangerous notion I am talking about, the notion that we understand our money, control it, and know what we want it to do for us. To date, however, no one has seriously challenged this notion and attempted to talk about money in the framework of our individual compulsions and anxieties.

No one has yet created an Alcoholics Anonymous for investors to help them understand what money means to them, what money is doing to them.

All of us are familiar with the compulsive gambler, the person who runs off to Vegas and risks job, family, everything, to make a big hit. But that's not what I am concerned about here. The obvious is visible to everyone. I am talking about something much broader and more fundamental. The reasoning goes like this:

Most, if not all, of us are compulsive to one extent or another; our individual compulsions affect our behavior in a variety of areas including the way we handle money; compulsiveness with money determines whether we handle it well or in a self-destructive manner. Once we understand the nature of our individual money mania, we can begin to do something about it, we can gain an insight into how others are exploiting us by manipulating our weaknesses, and we can turn losing behavior into winning behavior.

Perhaps what we need, after all, is some sort of *Investors Anonymous*, a place where we can freely air our personal idiosyncrasies about money without fear of being ridiculed. The disease is more widespread than you think. Comparatively few of us understand what money is and know how to manage it well. Those people are the exceptions. Investors Anonymous is for the great majority.

This book, then, is the first step in that direction.

CHAPTER TWO

Sharks and Barracudas

IT USUALLY BEGINS WITH your broker. In the language of the Street he (or she in increasing numbers now) is called a customer's man, an account executive, or a registered representative. Let's say he is with a bulwark of the financial world which we'll call Bull, Banks, Forbes & Trotsky to get around the legal problems. BBF&T for simplicity.

There is nothing wrong with stockbrokers that is not wrong with any other commission salesmen. The American system is built on competition and profits. Commissions are the incentives which major companies use to induce salesmen to move their particular products. The principle is the same whether the product is a vacuum cleaner, a set of encyclopedias, advertising time on radio and television, or stocks and bonds.

Say what you want about the system, it has provided us with a pretty decent standard of living. Americans have always had a soft spot in their hearts for the fast-talking hustler. Our folklore is filled with tales of quick-buck artists who can sell the Brooklyn Bridge to tourists or refrigerators to Eskimos. There is something uniquely American about the carny barker and the medicine man, about the W. C. Fields-type character, slightly crooked but lovable, who comes rambling down the road with a truckload of goods to unload upon the citizenry. Salesmanship is a legitimate craft in an economy which depends upon the give-and-take of the marketplace. While we have rules and regulations to protect the unwary against fraud and deceit, we have nevertheless been extremely tolerant of those with the ability to turn a fast profit from the quickness of their minds rather than the sweat of their brows.

The initial mistake most investors make is in regarding the broker as something other than he is. When the Avon lady comes calling at your door with a bagful of cosmetics, you don't consider her to be a fashion expert or a professional facial designer. She is a peddler of a company's products, nothing more or less. The same is true of the guy who wheels a brand-new Hoover up your driveway, or calls you on the phone and tells you that your children will turn into drooling illiterates unless you buy a four-hundred-dollar set of books from him.

With stockbrokers, however, the case is slightly different. While investors are aware that brokers earn their livings by generating commissions, they still regard them more as financial advisers or money managers than as salesmen. This is partly due to the nature of the product brokers are selling. They are dealing with money, which is more than just a tube of lipstick, more than just another vacuum cleaner or a new automobile. Brokers are people who know about MONEY and all that magic word represents. They are dealing in a commodity equally as mystifying as SEX and POWER and FOOD and ALCOHOL. Your broker is not selling you a tangible, easily recognizable need. He or she is trading in compulsion, anxiety, and mystery.

Your broker, if he is a smart, successful broker, understands you better than you do yourself. He understands your anxieties, develops your needs, and creates the product to fill them.

Look at it this way. If your car or vacuum cleaner breaks down for the sixth time in the last two months, you know you *need* a new car or vacuum cleaner to replace the old one. If your television screen looks like a Siberian landscape during a blizzard and no amount of repairing can fix it, you know you *need* a new television set.

But does anyone actually *need* 100 shares of General Motors? Does anyone *need* 300 Westinghouse at the market, or $10,000 worth of utility bonds? This is not to say that a few hundred shares of this, that, or something else may not be good for you. They all may go up and help you increase your store of MONEY and that is a measurable good. But *need* them? Not in the same way you need a machine to clean your house, a car to get to work, and even a TV set to help you keep your mental equilibrium from time to time.

Why not, for instance, RCA instead of GM; why not Texas bonds instead of Georgia; why not Union Electric Power instead of Portland General? The answer is that your broker is not really selling GM or RCA or CBS ad infinitum. He or she is selling something far more intangible than a piece of America. He is trading in fear, greed, anxiety, guilt, compulsion, and a few more mysterious products you probably never thought of.

If your broker is a successful broker, he is a better psychologist than you are aware of.

If you are like most investors, you first walk into the branch office of Bull, Banks, Forbes & Trotsky in the grip of a nagging and pervasive fear. You have a wad of money, perhaps $5,000, $10,000, or even $100,000. Whatever the amount, it means a great deal to you. You know the money would be safe in the bank, but you also know it could be employed better elsewhere to gain a bigger return. So you've decided to visit a broker and get some free advice.

You've heard all sorts of stories about what thieves brokers are. Their main interest is in whipping people's money in and out of the market, turning it over and over like flapjacks on a skillet, earning fat commissions for themselves. But you have to go *somewhere*, and brokers . . . well, brokers know about MONEY. Maybe you'll be lucky enough to find an honest broker, one with your best interests at heart.

You've chosen BBF&T because it is one of the giants in the brokerage industry. Its name is as widely recognized as the great arch of McDonald's, and just as all-American. How can you go wrong with BBF&T? How crooked can they be? Would McDonald's cheat you an ounce on their Big Mac? Would anyone steal your wallet in Disneyland?

Still, you are afraid. You have this small, medium, or king-sized pile of money, and you *don't want to lose it*. You want it to remain absolutely safe. You don't want some fast-talking hustler tricking you out of it, fattening his own wallet while he decimates yours. You are slightly paranoid and very much afraid as you walk up to the receptionist and ask to speak to a broker. But you need some advice and where else can you go? When you want to know about your health you go to a doctor. When you want financial advice you have to go to a money doctor, some sort of a financial G.P. BBF&T is as reputable as any of them. More so. Its logo is visible everywhere, as omnipresent as the flag.

The broker has been trained to know about all the things you can do with your money. He knows about such arcane subjects as money market instruments, munis, Ginnie Maes and Fanny Maes, P/E ratios, tax shelters, yields to maturity, and other magical phenomena that fill you with wonderment. Your broker had to pass a six-hour test dealing with all these matters before he received a license to operate.

After your broker passed the test and got his license, he was then thrown headlong into a highly competitive environment. He was given a desk, a telephone, and a secretary he had to share with three or four other brokers, and told to do some business. DO SOME BUSINESS! Call up people on the telephone and do some business. This is an environment where the success rate is extremely low, where the dropout rate exceeds 75 percent within the first two years.

Your broker learned very early in the game that his successful colleagues—unless they have family connections or other inroads to large pools of money—share certain characteristics. First of all, most of them are workaholics in the beginning. They come in early and work late two or three nights a week, sometimes on weekends. Second, they are highly motivated in their drive to make a great deal of money for *themselves* and their families. Third, they develop skins as thick as elephants' hides. They have the ability to take rejection on phone call after phone call, and still keep plunging ahead until they *do some business* on perhaps the fiftieth or sixtieth call of the day, long beyond the point where more sensitive spirits would have called it quits. Finally, the most successful brokers are excellent psychologists. More on this as we move along.

Lenny Harris and Gil Clark are both successful brokers. Lenny is known as a shark in the trade, and Gil is a barracuda. No matter how much money a client has invested with him, Lenny refuses to believe that there is not a hell of a lot more in reserve that the client is hiding from him.

"I know he's got more," Lenny says repeatedly about any given client. "The son of a bitch is burying it. If I don't dig it out of him now, somebody else'll get to it first."

Lenny is a shark because he believes in cleaning a client's bones until there is no more flesh remaining. Once he has a client hooked, he makes a notation on his calendar to call him back two weeks later to sell him something else. This is done repeatedly until the client screams, threatens to call the police, or begs for mercy. The shark school of brokerage is also known as back-and-fill; the broker goes back interminably and keeps filling the client's needs, which he created in the first place, until the client is either burned out or legitimately drained of surplus cash.

Gil Clark is more of a barracuda. Rather than concentrating on a few individuals at a time and cleaning their bones, Gil Clark prefers to take a bite out of many different clients. (I have no knowledge of the dining habits of sharks and barracudas, but this is the distinction given in the business.) Gil starts calling absolute strangers on the telephone as early as eight thirty in the morning, and keeps on dialing and smiling until as late as ten o'clock at night.

"It's sheer numbers," Gil admits. "It's strictly the law of

averages. If you talk to a hundred and fifty people a day, you've *got* to do some business."

If Lenny Harris's clients complain that they hear from their broker too much ("Every time I hear his voice I know he wants to sell me something"), Gil Clark's clients have the opposite lament ("Whenever I have a problem I can never get him on the phone. He puts me on hold and forgets about me").

This is no accident. Gil Clark's secretary is instructed to inquire of all callers whether or not they want to place an order. If the answer is yes, Gil naturally enough has time to talk to them. If it is no, or if a client has the audacity to call about a missing dividend check or to discuss a discrepancy on his latest statement, Gil puts him on hold until his hair turns white and the cobwebs start collecting on the receiver.

Aren't there any successful brokers who are neither sharks nor barracudas? Aren't there any honest brokers who are genuinely concerned about the anxieties and needs of their clients? Sure there are, lots of them. But they are in the minority. And they don't, as a rule, make nearly as much money as Lenny and Gil.

One of the most successful brokers at BBF&T is a gentleman named Dale Meredith Worthington. Dale is six feet two or three inches tall with a thick mat of wavy blond hair and large sky-blue eyes. He wears dark pinstriped suits, white shirts, black ties, and heavy wing-tip brogans. He is straight out of the pages of the old *Saturday Evening Post,* a regular God-fearing American Boy Scout, the backbone of the nation.

Dale Meredith Worthington bears an uncanny resemblance to the early Billy Graham and he is himself an ordained minister in the Baptist Church. His politics are as conservative as his taste in clothing and religion. When he is not singing the praises of Jesus and the American Way, he is sounding the trumpets for Ronald Reagan, the brothers Buckley, and other superstars of the ideological right.

Dale's clients are reflections of himself, as most brokers'

clients are. Brokers tend to attract clients with complementary neuroses, mirror images whom they understand well and work with successfully. Consequently, Dale's clients all seem to have been plucked from small rural farms circa 1890 or 1900. Where he ever found them in this day and age is difficult to say. Presumably there are still many of this kind to be found at Baptist picnics throughout the American heartland, but to see them visiting their golden-haired broker in midtown Manhattan is incongruous and unnerving. They exude an aura of potbellied stoves, fieldstone houses, rickety barns, wells and smokehouses, and hobnailed boots encrusted with chicken droppings. They travel seventy or eighty miles from the small New Jersey town where Dale lives, bringing him gifts straight from the oven: homemade bread, cakes, muffins, and cookies. Once an elderly hillbilly who could have been created by Norman Rockwell brought him an entire ham, smoked and cured in his own smokehouse, which Dale transported on the commuter express back to his home in New Jersey. Old ladies in funny hats, rimless glasses, black dresses, and thick black shoes which nuns won't wear any longer sit faithfully by his desk while Dale monologues them endlessly about the virtues of thrift, Jesus, Americanism, and God's plan for them to invest their dollars with him.

Around this folksy scene, the air is filled with voices as other brokers shout at their clients in English, Yiddish, Greek, Italian, Spanish, Chinese, and languages not yet identified. Yet, Dale Meredith Worthington and his born-again constituency seem oblivious to it all. They sit meekly and listen to Dale as his fire-and-brimstone voice rings out above the babble, his fingers stab the air in front of their faces to make a point; and his bright blue eyes hold them spellbound. The message is clear: giving your money to Dale is like paying your dues. It's doing your penance, cleaning the slate, tithing in church.

A session with their broker is a religious experience for Worthington's clients. It is a catharsis. They leave meek and humbled, comfortable in the knowledge that Jesus still loves them. They have tithed and their Maker smiles upon them. Dale logs the entry into his book. X amount of dollars from Mrs. So-and-so. Y amount from Mr. What's-his-name. Dale is unsmiling but he is evidently happy. It has been a good day's work. Dale Meredith Worthington is a Billy Graham lookalike with the soul of Barabbas. He is an extremely successful broker who manages to combine the attributes of both a shark and a barracuda in one awesome presence. While Lenny cleans the bones of a few individuals at a time and Gil takes a bite out of many different clients, Dale consumes the flesh *and* the bones of everyone he comes in contact with.

CHAPTER THREE

In the Grip of Fear and Greed

YOU HAVE NO WAY of knowing beforehand what kind of broker you will encounter on your first visit to BBF&T, but one thing is certain: whoever the broker is, he already knows more about you than you know about him. He can tell immediately whether you will make money or eventually lose it in the market.

If you are a winner, this will be evident at once and your broker will proceed accordingly. We'll discuss this sequence of events in Part Two. For the moment we are concerned about the losers.

Most seasoned brokers will tell you that they can tell within the first two minutes of a conversation whether or not a new client is going to be a winner or a loser. Some maintain they can smell the losers before they walk in the door. This is an important instinct to develop since the losers are better clients than investors who are in control of their passions. Every broker needs a steady stream of suckers to support the winners on his books.

Your new broker knows that your prevailing emotion is fear—fear and a paranoid suspicion. Since he is a salesman he will try to put you at ease. You need reassurance that you did the right thing in coming to him, and he understands this.

"How can I help you?" is the first question he will most likely ask you.

"I'm looking for a new broker," you might reply. "My last one was a dud. A nice guy, but a real bum. I'd've made a bundle if I did the opposite of everything he suggested."

Your new broker sits back and smiles reassuringly. He is sympathetic and full of understanding. He has you pegged already and you aren't even aware of it. He knows something you don't know: this is going to be a very rewarding relationship for him.

By far the most profitable clients for a broker to have are those who have been in the market before and lost a tidy sum. These are the people who have been investing over a period of, say, ten to twenty years, who start off smartly each time they come in only to get caught up in the newest craze and end up losing everything they have. They swear they have learned their lesson and will never get trapped again, and they are sincere in their intentions. But each time they come back into the market, the old pattern is resumed. Enter slowly, get suckered in deeper and deeper, take a plunge, and get wiped out. Every five years or so the cycle is repeated.

Your new broker, assuming he is a seasoned and successful broker, understands the cycle well. You are hopelessly caught up in the psychology of fear and greed. The syndrome is devastating. All of us are vulnerable and it is easy to fall prey to it from time to time. It takes an extremely self-disciplined, self-aware, and self-controlled individual to resist it.

Let's assume you have been in and out of the market for the past twenty years. You were invested rather heavily in the early seventies, and were wiped out in the crash of '74. Your portfolio of glamour stocks and fliers, at one time worth about $100,000, suddenly lost altitude, went into a nose dive, and crash landed at a net worth of $30,000—*$70,000* up in smoke, vanished into thin air just like that. You sold what you had left, grabbed your thirty grand and ran for the hills with your tail between your legs.

"Never!" you swore to yourself. "Never will I get burned like that again. Never will I let some fast-talking broker lead me down the garden path again. Never! I've learned my lesson this time. Never again!"

You were not alone in 1974. Millions of others just like you got killed. You heard the stories everywhere: $20,000 here, a hundred grand there, a *quarter of a million*. The amount of money lost in the debacle of 1974 was astronomical, absolutely incredible.

"Never again!" you vowed. You took your $30,000 and put it in the bank. A feeble investment, but safe. Nobody can get his hands on it there. It's tucked away forever.

In January of 1975 you saw the market rally sharply. It took off like a rocket and all those fallen giants—U.S. Steel, RCA, Polaroid, Eastman Kodak, ad infinitum—started to move again. "Oh, Christ!" you groaned. "I got out at the bottom. I panicked. *Shmuck!* If only I waited a little longer I could have salvaged more. Forty-five or fifty G's at least. Dummy. I panicked like an amateur. But that's it. Never again. It's too late now."

The rally of 1975 lasted until the end of June and then it fizzled. But what a comeback. From 600 at the beginning of 1975 the Dow Jones industrials soared back up to 875, a climb of nearly 50 percent. "Too late," you said. "I missed the boat. The hell with it. My money's staying in the bank." For the rest of 1975 the market roller-coasted up and down and ended the year at 850.

Then the gong went off in 1976 and, whammo!, the same thing happened all over again. The market started roaring like a raging bull and charged up 125 points by the end of January. At the end of March the DJIA touched the magical 1000 mark, and there it hovered, snaking between 950 and 1000, where it finished out the year.

"Good Christ almighty! This market's exploding all over the place," you wailed. "Everybody's making a fortune but me. Idiot! Dummy! Here I am collecting a miserable 5 percent in the bank and *everybody else is getting rich!*" All the economists, all the top analysts on the Street were predicting 1250 to 1300 by the end of 1977. The top man at Bull, Banks, Forbes & Trotsky was looking for another January rally, an explosion, a blast-off to the moon sometime during the next few months.

So here it is in late 1976, a scant two years since your disaster of 1974, and you decide to go back in. But this time you're going to be careful. This time it will be different. "No more Mr. Sucker. From now on it's Mr. Cautious. No broker is going to fatten up off my bones again. The institutions aren't going to leave me holding the bag this time around."

You enter the nearest branch office of BBF&T and, as the luck of the doomed would have it, you draw Lenny Harris as the broker of the day. He's the guy handling all new walk-in accounts on this particular day. You have no way of knowing this beforehand, of course, but Lenny subscribes to the shark school of brokerage: he cleans people's bones for a living. Lenny seems like a nice guy. He has a friendly smile and he dresses well. Haircut, shined shoes, pinstriped suit, the whole bit.

"My last broker was a bum," you tell him. "He couldn't pick a winning stock if it jumped up and danced on his head. This time I don't want to take any chances. No more risk. I've got about $20,000 I want to invest very conservatively. Good solid companies paying healthy dividends. No high fliers, understand?"

Lenny nods sympathetically, settles back in his chair, and threads his fingers behind his head. Deep inside he knows you are scared witless. He knows you are in thrall to a paranoid frenzy; you suspect him of being a crook, a thug, maybe even a rapist. He understands fear and paranoia. He works with them every day. All these observations, however, he keeps to himself. To you he says,

"Let me tell you how I work before we do any business. Just so we understand each other. First of all, I'm not a high-pressure guy. I have a very successful business and I don't believe in badgering people to earn my commissions. I don't *need* it. I have clients who are strictly buyers of tax-free bonds, others who don't mind taking a little risk once in a while, and I have my speculators. My files are cross-referenced so I don't mix them up. You tell me your objectives are preservation of capital, moderate growth and income, and I treat you accordingly. I don't try to talk people into taking risks they can't handle."

You nod appreciatively. This is what you came here for. Lenny sounds like an honest broker. At long last! He doesn't *need* you. He doesn't need to take your money and turn it over and over like hotcakes; he doesn't need to run you up and down like a yo-yo, to whip your hard-earned dollars round and round until you don't know where they are anymore; he doesn't need to churn you and burn you to make a living. Finally! An honest and successful broker. Aloof. A bit arrogant. Smart and successful. You're just a little guy compared to his other clients. He doesn't need your lousy twenty grand.

You're hooked and he knows it.

Lenny picks up his pen and asks you some questions. Married, children, good income, real estate and insurance, nothing too personal, mind you, just enough to get a handle on your financial needs and obligations.

"I would definitely suggest a more conservative approach for you this time around," says Lenny. "A utility paying a good tax-deferred dividend, and two or three solid companies with well-covered dividends and moderate growth potential." He recommends putting about $8,000 into San Diego Gas & Electric and another $8,000 into two good-quality growth stocks—RCA, which is selling around 25 or 26, and Texaco, in the same price range. Both companies pay respectable dividends and . . . well, how can you go wrong with these bedrocks of American industry? The income alone from these investments will give you much more than the bank pays, and Lenny wants you—no, he *insists* that you keep $4,000 in reserve as a cushion.

"In addition to the extra income," says Lenny, "I'm looking for 29 or 30 on RCA and 32 to 34 on Texaco within the next six months."

Lenny has succeeded in overcoming your fear and, at this point, you almost feel a little guilty about holding back the other $10,000 from him. You decide to go ahead—$8,000 into San Diego and 150 shares each of RCA and Texaco. You're back into the market again, but this time you're doing it right.

No more Mr. Sucker. From now on you're going to be smart. Lenny opens an account for you and writes up the trades.

"By the way," you can't resist asking before you take your leave, "I read where one of your top analysts is looking for another New Year rally in January. What do you think?"

"I take all that with a grain of salt," says Lenny. "I'm neutral on the short-term but very bullish long-term. Give it five to six months at least and I think you'll see some results." You're not aware of it, but brokers are *always* neutral near-term and optimistic long-term. This is the safest position since it gives them some breathing room if the stocks they've just put you into come down with the Siberian flu.

"Well"—your voice becomes a shade more confidential—"I may have a few more dollars coming in next month. Not much, a couple of thousand or so. If you hear of anything *real good*, give me a call."

"That's not for you," Lenny snaps. "I don't want you to get into something you can't live with, something that's going to keep you awake at night."

"Well, I don't mind taking a small gamble with a couple of grand," you say. "If you hear of something *really hot,* I mean."

"I'll keep you in mind," he says as he reaches for the phone. He obviously has more pressing business to attend to now. Somewhat apologetically you get up and shake his hand. He is already talking into the phone to one of his other clients about a "special situation" before you leave the office.

Not only does another New Year rally fail to materialize in January, 1977, but the market begins to head south for the winter. It starts a steady decline right from the opening bell and continues to fall all the way through a dull, lackluster year. Still, you are not doing badly. The dividend checks are steady and RCA is actually rising in a falling market, bucking the overall trend. It makes 28, then falls back to 26. In March it's up to 30 but by April it's back down to 27½. In May it pushes up through 30 and makes it to 31.

You're on the phone every two weeks or so with Lenny. The man's a bloody genius to give you action like this in such a lousy market. He *knows* things. Texaco is a bit anemic, but at least it's holding its own. Not once did it fall below your purchase price and it actually touched 30 before dropping back to 26.

"What do you think?" you ask Lenny. By this time you're beginning to trust him a little. Not only is he preserving your capital in a falling market, but you're even up a bit.

"I was looking for more on Texaco," he says one day in June, "but now I'm not so sure. This goddamn market just won't cooperate."

"What do you *think*? Should I sell them now? Do you see anything else that looks *good*?"

"I hear things all the time," he says confidentially. "But I'm not sure they're for you. They're not for the conservative investor."

"I don't mind taking a little risk. RCA and Texaco have both been good. Not spectacular, mind you. But we do have some small profits. What do you *think*?"

"Look. Here's what we'll do. Hang on to your San Diego. The income is good and there's a tax advantage, so let's leave that alone. I'd like to see you take your profits in the other two and put the money in something else. Are you sure you can handle this?"

"What? What else? What do you hear?"

"Are you sure you want to go this route?"

At this point you have been back in the market six months again. Your initial fear is all but dissipated. You and Lenny have established a chatty relationship and he has lived up to his early promise: he has not tried to high-pressure you into anything. He calls you every two weeks or so, or sometimes you call him. You talk about politics (brokers, like most salesmen, usually agree with their clients' politics, whatever they happen to be), the weather, your kids, his kids, and incidently about the profits you have in your stocks while the overall market is skidding further southward. Your fear of six months back has given way to a hint of greed. Not chronic greed. After all, nobody is making much money in this market. But Lenny has called a couple of good turns for you so far, and the old dormant greed is beginning to stir again. Lenny doesn't want to hurt you but he can smell your mounting greed before you're even aware of it. His antennae quiver automatically. He has nothing to do with it; no conscious decision has been made on his part. But the smell of money is in the air and his response is Pavlovian. His sixth sense is in gear. The killer instinct is on automatic pilot.

"I told you back in December that I hear things from time to time." And so he does. He's talking to people all the time. He doesn't deliberately want to hurt you or anybody else for that matter. He would like nothing better than to pick one winning stock after another. He may even have some of his own money in a stock he is recommending. The more winners he picks, the more money both he and his clients make. If he can put you into one successful trade after another, then everybody comes out ahead. The best of all possible worlds.

"What are you onto?" you ask.

"Revlon. New product they're coming out with sometime in the fall. Could be a doubler. Now's the time to get into it. The stock is 40 now, could be 70 or 80 in October."

You're sweating now. Your hands are sticky and your body heat is steaming up your glasses. Oh, my God! Not all over again. Never again!

"Are—are you sure?"

"Sure? I'm not sure I'll be alive tomorrow morning. Maybe the government will collapse and we'll all be starving in the streets. What's sure?" Lenny is almost shrieking. Then his voice grows calmer and lower. "But like I told you, I hear things. Maybe this is not for you. Maybe you should stay put and at least sleep well at night."

"What—what kind of a dividend does it pay?"

"Dividend!" Lenny spits this out like you've just said a dirty word. Suddenly dividends are garbage. "You're not in this for the dividend. This is a mover, I'm telling you. If you're looking for dividends buy some more San Diego. Buy Long Island Lighting. Buy American Electric Power."

The sweat is cascading in rivulets down your chest and back.

"So—so what do you think?" you ask.

"Take your profits and put them into Revlon."

"Do—do it."

"Done! Sell 150 Texaco and 150 RCA at the market and pick up 225 shares of Revlon." He had it worked out to the nickel before he even called you. Mind like a steel trap, that Lenny. "I'll call you later with the prices."

So you sell your RCA at 31 and Texaco at 29 and buy 225 Revlon at 40. Not bad. You feel better already. Your $8,000 investment in these two stocks has grown by $1,000, and you now own $9,000 worth of Revlon. Minus commissions, of course. But what the hell. He's making money for you, so why shouldn't he make a few dollars for himself? You're up 12 percent in six months, and that doesn't include the dividends, which were substantial. You have only one regret as you hang up the phone:

If Revlon is going to double in four months, maybe you should have sold your San Diego and bought 400 shares instead. Maybe you should have taken the other fourteen grand out of the bank and gone in for, let's see, 700 or 750 shares. If you hadn't panicked in 1974 you could have picked up 1000 shares today and run it up to $80,000 by October. *Shmuck!* Sold out at the bottom with all the other assholes. Never again. From now on it's Mr. Smart.

From this point on your relationship with Lenny changes substantially. Now you are on the phone with him once or twice a day instead of once every two or three weeks. Lenny is never too busy to give you quotes when you call.

"Revlon's up to 43," he tells you one day in August. "The stock's up 3 points and the rest of the market's in the crapper.

There's too much overall selling pressure."

"Do you still see 70 or 80 by October?" you question timidly. After all, 3 points is 3 points, but 30 or 40 is a whole different ballgame.

"If we get the right kind of market the stock can hit 100. The conditions have to be just right."

"What's wrong with the market? What's holding it back?"

"Hard to say. The institutions keep dumping big blocks. Every time we get a bounce they grab some quick profits and sit on the sidelines."

"How about your man downtown? Is he still looking for 1200 by September?"

"He's turned a bit more bearish. Worried about rising interest rates and a possible recession next year. He does think we'll get a late-summer rally, though. A blast-off of 100 points or so to about 1050 or 1100."

"What—what do *you* think?"

"I want you to hang in there a few more weeks with Revlon. The stock's acting well in a dull market. It should lead the rest of the market when we get our rally."

Two weeks later you get an urgent call from Lenny. He's got something very important to discuss with you.

"I want you to sell your Revlon and switch into Westinghouse," he says.

"Wh—what's wrong with Revlon?"

"Wrong? Nothing's wrong. The stock just hit 44. You're up 10 percent since June and the rest of the market's sitting there like a big blob."

"But you said 70 or 80 by October."

"In the *right kind* of market, I said. I can't fight the institutions, can I? You're up 10 percent in three months, 25 percent on the year so far when everybody else is losing a *fortune*, and you're complaining."

"I'm not complaining. I just thought . . . Look, you're doing a terrific job, no complaints, all right. I—"

"*We're* making money in a down market. *We're* making the

right moves and *we're* way ahead of the game. I'm trying to make back some of that money you lost in '74."

"Hey, look, I'm not complaining. If you think Westinghouse is a good move right now we'll make the switch."

"It's the *smart* move right now, believe me."

"What do you hear?"

"Like I said, I hear things all the time. I can't go into details, but I *hear* things."

"But isn't Westinghouse having all kinds of problems with uranium claims?"

"That's the whole point. The stock is down from 22 since June. We can pick it up at 17 now. According to my information," he says confidentially, "it's definitely a turnaround situation."

"How—how much of a move?" you dare to ask.

"By December it'll be 25 to 30. It's a steal right now under 20. And it's a lower-priced stock than Revlon. You can go in for 500 shares. Look at the leverage. Every time it moves a point you make $500."

"You're sure?"

"Sure? How can I be sure I'll even be alive tomorrow morning? Maybe the Russians'll bomb us and we'll all be blown to smithereens. That's the end of the ballgame for everyone."

"Take it easy. I just want to be careful, that's all."

"*We* can't go wrong with Westinghouse at 17," he says calmly now. "It's *screaming* to be bought. I'm telling you, the stock is good for 25 to 30 in the near term."

That other $14,000 you've been hiding in the bank until now has been burning a hole in your passbook. A lousy 5 percent on all that money.

"Look," you say to Lenny. "If you think Westinghouse is that good, maybe I should go in for 1,000 shares. What do you think?"

"How much did you want to put in?" He throws the ball back to your court.

"Well, I've got about $9,000 I can spare right now."

"Why not buy 2,000 shares on margin? Look at the leverage you'll have."

"M—margin." You almost gag on the word. You were on margin in 1974. Never again! No more Mr. Idiot!

"Only if you can live with it," says Lenny. "I don't want you to lose any sleep at night."

"Let's just stick to the 1,000 shares," you apologize.

"Done! Sell 225 shares of Revlon at the market and buy 1,000 Westinghouse. I'll call you later with the prices."

You feel good after you hang up the phone. You managed to turn $8,000 into nearly $10,000 in nine months, and you're earning fat dividend checks from the San Diego Gas & Electric. Not only that, but you successfully resisted Lenny's suggestion that you go on margin. You're playing it smart this time around. No more margin, no more being bullied by a broker. Lenny is calling the turns right so far, even though you didn't double your money with the Revlon. At least you're making money.

A few weeks later Lenny wants to get you out of Westinghouse at 18½.

"But you said 25 to 30."

"This goddamn market just won't cooperate. What are you complaining about, anyway? You'll net over $1,000 after commissions and the market is on its ass. Who else has a track record like that this year? Besides . . ."—Lenny pauses for effect, then resumes more slowly—"you asked me to let you know if I ever hear of something *real hot*. Well, I'm onto a *special situation*."

"Better than Westinghouse?"

"I still think you can get 25 for Westinghouse if you're willing to sit on the sidelines for another six months in this crummy market," he says coldly. "But I thought you were looking for a fast mover, a *special situation*."

"What do you hear?" You're beginning to sweat a bit again.

"Possible takeover candidate. Are you interested?"

"Wh—what is it?"

"Pop Shoppes. A fast-food chain trading over the counter."

"A takeover candidate?"

"That's what I hear."

"Are you sure?"

"Sure? How can I be sure the goddamn Chinese won't launch a missile at us tomorrow morning? How can I be sure I won't drop dead—"

"Okay, okay. So what do you think?"

"We'll sell 1,000 Westinghouse at 18½ and buy 3,000 Pop Shoppes around $6 a share."

"What do you hear on the takeover? How much?"

"Could be 12 to 15. At least a doubler."

You do some quick mental arithmetic and come up with a figure.

"I've been thinking, Lenny."

"About what?"

"This San Diego Gas & Electric. It pays a nice dividend, but it's not going anywhere."

"What do you want from a utility? You buy them for income. If you're looking for action they're not for you."

"The checks are nice but . . . this Pop Shoppes. You think it really can move?"

"That's what I'm telling you. I *hear* things from time to time."

"Suppose we sell the San Diego and put the money into this Pop Shoppes too. What do you think?"

"Is that what *you* want to do?"

"You think it can double, right?"

"I hear things. What can I tell you?"

"Okay." You're sweating like a pig now, but when you add up the numbers it's enough to give you palpitations. Recoup your losses from 1974. Make a bundle and retire early. Never work again. My God almighty! It's too much to contemplate.

"Do it, Lenny."

"Done! Sell 1,000 Westinghouse and 500 San Diego and buy 4,000 Pop Shoppes. I'll get back to you later."

When you hang up the phone you suddenly realize you've got over $24,000 tied up in Pop Shoppes. *Twenty-four thousand dollars! Pop Shoppes!* What in Christ's name is a Pop Shoppe anyway? You're back on the phone to Lenny first thing in the morning.

"Lenny, this Pip Pop, Pop Pop, I mean this Pop Shoppes of yours."

"What about it?"

"Well, uh, where are they located anyway?"

"Located? I, um, let me see, I think they're out in the Midwest somewhere. Yeah, that's it. Out in the Midwest."

"The Midwest? And, uh, what kind of a chain is it? Fast food or what?"

"Um, I think they're in health food. That's it, yogurt and vitamins."

"You—you hear any more about this takeover?"

"Look, I'm tied up on another line right now. Give it a few weeks or so, okay? I'll call you next week."

"Lenny, you're sure this information is reliable, right?"

"I'm on *long distance*, for Christ's sake! Give it two or three weeks to work out, okay? It's a good move, don't worry. I gotta ring off now."

So Lenny rings off and all you know is that you own $24,000 worth of a company that sells yogurt and vitamins somewhere in the Midwest. Imbecile! Your own broker doesn't know any more about the outfit than you do. Oh, my God! You panic. I'm going to get killed again.

A week goes by and Pop Shoppes is trading at 5¾–6½ on an average volume of 400 shares a day. The spread, the market! It's so *thin*.

"Lenny, I'm worried."

More and more Lenny puts you on hold when you call. He has his secretary give you quotes instead of getting on himself. Lenny seems to be *avoiding* you.

Two months go by and Pop Shoppes is trading at 5–5¾. The spread is still enormous and the volume is nowhere. You're getting nickeled-and-dimed to death and Lenny won't return your calls. Even his secretary puts you on hold now. One day you read an article in *The Wall Street Journal* about Pop Shoppes. It's a soda-pop chain headquartered in New Jersey. Not yogurt in the Midwest—root beer in New Jersey. And yes, it's true, some conglomerate has shown interest in acquiring the company. A major brokerage firm puts a buy on the stock for the first time ever. The volume picks up and the price starts to move: 5½–6¼; 5¾–6½. The spread is narrowing: 6¼–6¾; 6¾–7¼; 7–7¼.

Brrring! Your phone rings. It's Lenny. His first call to you in three months.

"Have you been following Pop Shoppes?" he asks nonchalantly, as though he spoke to you only yesterday.

Have you been following Pop Shoppes? You've been staying awake with the stock every night for weeks on end.

"It's moving," you squeal. It's finally happening. A doubler. Your ship has come in at long last. Easy Street from now on. You're going to be rich.

"If we sell now you'll net about $3,500," Lenny says. "I've got a *real special deal* I heard about just this morning."

"Sell!" He must be crazy. This one's going to the moon. What the hell is he talking about? "Sell already? You said 12 to 15."

"That was three months ago. Situations change. You might get 7½ or 8 if you're willing to wait another week or two, but if this takeover deal doesn't go through, the stock can fall apart."

This time you're not going to be bullied. This time you'll stand your ground. Who does he think he is anyway? Trying to talk you out of a fortune. Hasn't called you in months and now he's trying to churn you into something else.

"I think I'll hold," you say firmly. "I'm sure I can get 9 or 10 out of this one at least."

"You're the boss," he says. "Call me if you need any help."

The stock holds at 7 bid for another week and a half, then something happens. Large volume on the sell side. It begins to slip—6½–7; 6¼–6¾. You start to panic. Oh my God! I might get wiped out! You call Lenny.

"What's happening?"

"I told you to sell at 7."

"But what's *happening?*"

"Looks like the deal fell through like I warned you. What do you want to do?"

What do *I* want to do?

"What do *you* think?"

"I want you to roll over into Polaroid."

"Polaroid? Why?"

"I hear things. I keep on telling you."

You're almost crying now. "Okay. Get me out at 6¼. That way I'll just about break even."

"I'll do the best I can," he says. "The market's fading fast."

Lenny sells 500 shares at 6¼, 1,000 more at 6, and the other 2,500 between 5½ and 5¾. With commissions out, you've lost over $1,000 for the first time since coming back into the market. Not a wipeout, but enough to make you cautious again. You blame Lenny.

"You said 12 to 15."

"I told you to sell at 7." He tosses the ball back to you. "Either you call the shots or I do. There's no middle ground."

You feel you've won the argument, but you're also the one who has lost the money. Not him. Arguments he's willing to concede, but not commissions.

"I want to be more careful next time," you say.

"You're the boss," says Lenny.

"That Pop Shoppes was a bit too speculative. I'm still looking for a mover, but something a little more on the conservative side."

"Buy Polaroid," says Lenny.

"You're sure?"

"Sure!" he screams.

So you buy 1,000 shares of Polaroid at 23½. How can you

go wrong with Polaroid, a pillar of American technology and know-how, a regular household word?

The market hangs around in the doldrums for week after week, a month and more. You're not getting hurt, but neither are you making any money. The dividend on Polaroid is puny compared to the one you were collecting on San Diego Gas & Electric, and the stock is just sitting there going nowhere. Hell, you would be doing better with your money in the bank the way things have been going lately.

And then one day in the spring of 1978 something dramatic happens. On a Friday when most people are making plans for the weekend, the market suddenly explodes without warning. The eruption is enormous, Mount Vesuvius gone beserk. A tidal wave of dollars comes flooding into the market, driving prices up on record high volume. No one knows exactly where the money is coming from, but buying reaches panic proportions. The big issues lead the advance and Polaroid is among them.

Your phone rings early in the afternoon. Somehow you know who it is before you answer it. Lenny. He hasn't called you in six weeks but you know it's him. You can *feel* it.

"All hell is breaking loose," he exclaims. He sounds euphoric. "This is what I've been waiting for, the big breakout. I knew it was coming. I could feel it in my bones."

"How come?"

"It had to happen sooner or later. There was too much cash sitting on the sidelines, too many good buys around. It was only a question of when."

"How long will it last? What do you think?"

"Who knows? Could be a short ride but I don't think so. Meanwhile, Polaroid is jumping like a rabbit. *We're* making money."

The boredom of the past few months is forgotten on the spot. The doubts you had about taking money out of the bank and committing it to the market are swept away in the frenzy of the moment. Of course the market had to explode. It always does sooner or later. How could you have doubted it for a moment? It was only a question of when. Five percent in the bank at a time like this? You've got to be kidding.

Monday morning the buying panic continues. Each day new records are set. Fifty, sixty million shares a day; where will it end? Some analysts are predicting 80-million-share days just around the corner.

Meanwhile, your store of MONEY is growing rapidly. Twenty-three thousand dollars' worth of Polaroid has zoomed to $28,000. Then to $33,000. Fantastic! Where else can your money grow like this? Where else can you make $3,000 or $4,000 a day just by sitting home and reading the paper? It's MAGIC. Now you know you've done the right thing. Five percent in the bank? Nine percent on a utility? Who needs it? This is *real* money. This is the smart way to invest. Let the assholes wait forever to double their money. You're going to double yours overnight, maybe even triple it. Or more. Who knows? This is the action you've been waiting for.

The buying continues and Polaroid is up to 36. A beautiful move, but there is only one thing wrong: *it's not climbing fast enough.* The real moves are in the gambling stocks, particularly Resorts International A and B—13, 14, 15 points a day! People are making fortunes every day, and your stock is up only 12 or 13 points in three weeks.

You hear all kinds of stories about the fortunes being amassed in Resorts International. Gambling fever has exploded in America in epidemic proportions. Legalized gambling in Atlantic City and Resorts is the first one on the scene. Miami will be next and then New York state. The experts are predicting a dozen or more states will legalize gambling during the next two years. Just think of the profits. Just think of all the MONEY.

Your sister knows a guy who heard about this cab driver who put his entire life savings in Resorts International a year ago. He bought 4,000 shares of the Class A stock at $8 a share, a total of $32,000, every nickel he had in the world. And now Resorts is $70 a share and still climbing. It's up over 100. People are shorting the stock and getting killed: 120 on Resorts A and 190 on the B. The cabbie is worth, oh, my God, $480,000 now. He'll never have to push a hack again, never have to cart abusive drunks around the city for the rest of his life. Did he sell yet? Hell, no. The way that stock is climbing, he figures he'll be worth a million in a month or so.

And there you are with your lousy $36,000 worth of Polaroid. *Hundreds of thousands* are being made by taxicab drivers, and you're up only $13,000 in a market like this. You call Lenny.

"Where's Polaroid?"

"Thirty-eight. We're rolling now. This market doesn't want to quit."

"Lenny, what do you think of Resorts International?"

"Resorts? It's made its big move already. I'd stay away from it."

So you stay away and the next day Resorts A and B are up another 14 and 19 points respectively. Idiot! Fortunes are being made and you're stuck with a dog like Polaroid. Fifteen lousy points in a market that's gone berserk. You call Lenny.

"Do you know how much money I lost last week?" you ask.

"What are you talking about? Polaroid's up to 40."

"You told me not to buy Resorts and it's up another 35 points. My cousin Bill made $10,000 last week. My mailman made $18,000." You tell him about the cab driver with 4,000 shares. He's worth, Jesus Christ, almost $700,000 in a year. Now *that's* an investment.

Lenny is exasperated. "Look. I've never seen anything like this in my life. The stock's going to fall like a rock one of these days. When it falls it'll be down 20 and 30 points a day. They'll stop trading the goddamn thing and open it up at 8 again."

The next day Resorts A is up to $200 a share and the B is up near $300. That's another fortune Lenny lost you overnight. You call him up first thing in the morning.

"Eight hundred thousand that cab driver is worth now. A lousy cabbie is almost a millionaire and here I am with Polaroid."

Lenny is on the defensive now. He feels like a fool because he can't argue with your figures. You're absolutely right. And it's not only Resorts International. Other gambling issues have been roaring to the moon as well: Caesar's World, Bally, King International, Golden Nugget, Del Webb. The motel chains with interests in Atlantic City are also getting a big play. Even the utility serving the area, Atlantic City Electric, moved up 5 points one day. Lunacy! Lenny knows from past experience that the bubble has to burst sooner or later. The fall has to come and it will be a hard one. A lot of people who can't afford it are going to be clobbered. But you've put him in a trap. The madness continues and fortunes are being made in a matter of days. This bedlam might last for another month, six months even, before the collapse.

"What do you think?" you ask Lenny.

"I'm a little bit afraid of Resorts now," he says. "It's made such an enormous move already."

"How about some of the others? How about Caesar's World, Bally, Ramada? How about Howard Johnson or Holiday Inns?"

"Why don't we do this? Polaroid is up to 55. We've got a huge profit there, over $30,000. Why don't we take it now and roll it into Bally, which is also around the same price."

"You like Bally, hah?"

Lenny's firm recently put a buy on Bally. The top analysts had missed the boat on the gambling stocks, as did most Street analysts, and were embarrassed because of it. They did the best they could to dampen the fever by planting scare stories. Robert Metz did a hatchet job on Resorts in *The New York Times*, and Charles Elia did the same in *The Wall Street Journal*. These articles slowed the action for a day or so, but the frenzy continued. Nothing could kill it. Finally, after Bally had zoomed from 15 to 40, Bull, Banks, Forbes & Trotsky did a favorable write-up on the gambling industry and singled out Bally Manufacturing as the one to buy now. Lenny at least had some analytical support on this issue.

"Yes, I like Bally," he says, becoming the salesman again. "Of all of them, I think Bally has the best chance of becoming the *next Resorts International*."

Magic! Bells! Jackpot! The *next* Resorts. Everyone's looking for the next Resorts and now you've found it.

"You're sure?"

"Sure? How can I be—"

"All right. I just want to be careful. How far can it go?"

"Who knows?" says Lenny, back in control again. "Look at Resorts. From nickels and dimes to $300 a share."

"You think Bally can make 300?"

"Why not? Resorts did it, right?"

"Do it."

"Done! Sell 1,000 Polaroid at the market and buy 1,000 Bally."

"Lenny."

"Yes?"

"Make it 2,000 Bally. I'll buy it on margin."

CHAPTER FOUR

A Margin of Guilt

THE REST, AS THEY SAY, is history. Bally made it to 71¾ before the bottom fell out. Resorts was the first to break and the others quickly followed in its wake.

What finally caused the collapse?

It is difficult to pinpoint a single cause, as it always is in these cases. Miami voted against legalized gambling in the November referendum. Newspapers printed stories about mob connections to the gaming industry, and there was talk of holding up licenses for Resorts, Caesar's, and the other companies pending an investigation.

But all this was known beforehand. Polls showed gambling going down to defeat in Miami weeks ahead of time, and even your innocent neighborhood nun was aware that racketeers gravitated to gambling like so many flies around a fruitcake. None of this was a surprise. Most investors with money in the gaming issues took a very cavalier attitude when reporters warned of Mafia control.

"So what?" was the typical response. "The state gets a percentage, the mob takes a cut, and there's still a bundle left over for the stockholders. The mob isn't stupid. They're not going to destroy a good thing completely. Gambling is always going to be a lucrative business."

The logic was fine. The mob takes a cut from the Las Vegas action, too, but the casinos continue to make more and more money each year. So what if the voters in Miami turned down gambling? Sooner or later they would have to accept it and dozens of other states would also have to legalize it. It made good economic sense. Gambling was an industry whose time had come. Cities facing deficits could no longer afford to say no to the potential new revenue.

The market collapsed because it always collapses sooner or later after a fast and substantial advance. Investors take profits and prices come tumbling down. And when they did, starting in the early fall of 1978, the gambling stocks fell the fastest. They had risen quicker than anything else and had the longest way to drop. This is the basic law of the marketplace and it is effective most of the time. There are occasional exceptions, but they are extremely rare.

When stock prices fell in the last quarter of the year, those who had bought on margin were hit the hardest. Margin calls were coming in every day, and those who did not have the cash to meet them found their stocks being sold out from under them at lower and lower prices.

The mathematics works like this: Let's assume you bought $50,000 worth of stocks on margin. With the requirements in effect in 1978, you had to put up 50 percent or $25,000 for the stocks. This means the brokerage firm lent you the other $25,000 at constantly rising interest rates which soared over 13 percent by the end of the year.

> You bought $50,000 worth of stocks
> You borrowed $25,000 @ 10, 11, 12, then 13 percent
> Your equity was $25,000

The rules set by most brokerage firms require you to maintain an equity of 30 percent of the market value of the stocks. If your equity falls below this figure, you start to get margin calls. So let's say the value of your stocks declined to $40,000 a month after you bought them. This is how your position looked.

> Market value $40,000
> Debit $25,000
> Equity $15,000
> Maintenance requirement $12,000 (30 percent of the market value)

Three weeks passed and the sell-off continued at a harrowing pace. Doomsday! Everybody from the lowliest college professor to the president's top economic adviser was predicting a recession in 1979. Carter's chief inflation fighter even used the word *depression*. Your stocks continued to plummet with the rest.

                   Market value $35,000
                          Debit $25,000 (and growing with the interest
                         Equity $10,000   charges)
         Maintenance requirement $10,500

At this point you were within $500 of getting your first margin call. You hadn't perspired like this since 1974. Please, God, if there is a God, make the market bottom out. Give us a rally, a bounce, a sign, something. The selling continued into November and the DJIA fell below 800.

                   Market value $30,000
                          Debit $25,000
                         Equity $ 5,000
         Maintenance requirement $ 9,000
                    Margin call $ 4,000

Now you had to do one of two things. You could have dipped back into your piggy bank and come up with another $4,000 in cash, assuming you had it available with Christmas and the holiday season approaching and your expenses mounting, or, failing this, your broker had to sell off *$13,334* worth of stock to meet the $4,000 margin call.

Why $13,334 instead of only $4,000 worth of stock? Because according to the rules, only 30 percent of the sale of stock can be released to cover a call. Consequently, your broker is required to sell 3⅓ times the amount of the call.

         Market value after the sale $16,666
                          Debit $11,666
                         Equity $ 5,000
         Maintenance requirement $ 5,000
                     Margin call $ 0

Within the next two weeks the value of your stocks declined another $4,000.

Market value $12,666
Debt $11,666
—————
Equity $ 1,000
Maintenance requirement $ 3,800
Margin call $ 2,800

The market fell again and three weeks later you were totally wiped out. BBF&T retrieved the $25,000 it lent you plus a healthy vigorish, and you wound up with zero. In reality, the sell-off of your stocks would have occurred in smaller stages: $700 here, another $1,000, perhaps $450 a few days later until your equity was whittled away in slices like a salami.

Shmuck! You did it again. You repeated the disaster of 1974. Those heavily invested in gambling stocks found their positions obliterated fastest, with new margin calls coming in literally every day.

BBF&T, Lenny, Gil, and Dale made out just fine and you struck out again. BBF&T got all its money back with interest. In addition, your broker and his firm generated commissions when you bought the stock in the beginning and each time you were forced to sell off stock thereafter.

Does this mean that your broker and his firm had no compassion for their clients? Not at all. In early December of 1978 Bull, Banks, Forbes & Trotsky had one of their analysts write a paper concerning the heavy margin selling that had been going on for the past two and a half months. The analyst concluded that the clients of BBF&T and other brokerage firms had gone too deeply into debt. He recommended that they reduce their margin exposure immediately to eliminate additional forced selling in the future.

Pity that the study hadn't been released in September instead of December. Then again, who would have listened anyway in the midst of a bull market?

*   *   *

Investors who bought their stocks for cash, that is, paid for them in full, were at least in a position to ride out the sell-off and wait for the next up-cycle to begin. A paper loss of $20,000 on an investment of $50,000 is still only a paper loss. You own the stocks outright and can, therefore, maintain your position without being forced to sell stocks at lower and lower prices. You can sit back and wait out the panic without biting your nails down to the bone.

Brokers, on the other hand, are not only under pressure to buy and sell stocks; there is also a strong incentive to put their clients on margin. Margin, as we have just seen, is good for the brokerage firm and it is good for the broker. An investor with $25,000 can buy $50,000 worth of stocks through the MAGIC OF MARGIN. And the commissions on $50,000 worth of stocks are nearly double the commissions on half that amount.

You understood all this before you came back into the market again toward the end of 1976. You had been through it before once, twice, several times, and each time you swore it would never happen again. Each time you took the pledge and stuck to it for a while, only to fall off the wagon repeatedly.

By the end of 1978 you swore you were finished with the market forever this time. No more BBF&T's, no more Lennys, Gils, Dales, or any other hotshot brokers. This time you really meant it and you told Lenny so. Lenny didn't believe you, though. He knows you will be back, maybe not in 1979 or 1980, but certainly by 1981 or so. Just as soon as the merry-go-round starts again and the newest craze sets in, whatever it happens to be at the time. The fear-greed syndrome is too powerful for most investors to ignore. Most of us find it difficult to avoid, almost impossible to resist when fortunes are made by people around us and we seem to be the only ones who missed the boat.

What most of us fail to realize, however, is that the so-called fortunes being made by other investors are few and far between. Much of it is on paper only and most people fail to take their profits on time. The cabbie waiting for his Resorts International to reach a cool million never quite made it. He rode his bundle up to a shade over $800,000 before the market collapsed. While he is now worth a lot more than he was at the start, he still hasn't sold to lock in his profit. He'll never settle for a lousy $300,000 when he knew he was worth more than twice as much as that at one time. Chances are he wouldn't have sold for $1 million even if he could have. Like most of us he would have figured that, since the first million bucks was so easy, he might as well hang on for a million and a half. Hell, $2 million is right around the corner. No?

Likewise, those of us who swear we will take our profit and run, if only we can double our money, invariably insist on tripling the investment once the initial goal has been reached. Then tripling it is not enough. Why not wait until we have quadrupled or quintupled our stake?

What is enough anyway? Nothing is ever enough. There is no such thing as enough where money is concerned because, no matter how much we have, someone always has more than we do. Money is not even the key issue after a while. If it were, anybody would have to be crazy to turn down $800,000 when it was available. Even $300,000 for that matter.

No, it's not really the money. It's MAGIC. Fear and greed. Compulsion. Craziness. An almost unbreakable cycle. A need to *be somebody*, to find the Magic Kingdom, Utopia, Salvation, a need to be looked upon as somebody special by others. An obsession which invariably ends up in bitter self-destruction.

Fear. Greed. Compulsion. Magic. And then there is guilt!

Joe Ferguson had never been in the market before. He never had any money to speak of until the last couple of years.

In 1969 he got married for the first time. His bride was the daughter of an Irish immigrant named McBride who came to New York in 1922 and opened a bar in a working-class neighborhood. Let's say the bar was called McBride's Irish Soldier, and it caught on immediately. It was a very popular place for cops, firemen, construction workers, and other laborers to lift a glass and get a good meal at low prices.

McBride made a lot of money and opened another Irish Soldier bar, then another and another in various parts of New York City. In twenty years he had developed a chain of McBride's Irish Soldier bars, all of them raking in money faster than he could spend it. Old man McBride was worth several million dollars by the mid-1950's.

When Ferguson married the Irish Soldier heiress he quit his job as a New York City fireman and went to work managing one of his father-in-law's establishments in the Bronx. Three years later he bought the place from the old man, then opened a second bar on his own in midtown Manhattan. Since he was in a cash business he did what most crafty entrepreneurs do: he hid most of his income from IRS and tucked it away in his safe-deposit box. As far as IRS was concerned, Joe Ferguson reported a salary of $25,000 a year which he took from his corporation, and this is the amount he paid taxes on. No one except his wife, his brother, and a few trusted friends knew that he was stashing another $600 to $700 a week in his iron box.

The only difference between Joe Ferguson and most other proprietors of a cash business was that Joe felt *guilty* about what he was doing.

In the summer of 1976 Ferguson decided that he needed some financial assistance. What was he going to *do* with all this money he had hidden? How could he invest it in a way that he could at least earn some interest on it? He couldn't suddenly deposit over $100,000 in cash in his savings account. He had heard somewhere that banks were required to notify IRS of any suspicious transactions, and how could he account for all this legal tender on a $25,000 annual income which was allegedly supporting a wife and four children in an expensive house in Riverdale?

So Joe looked up an old friend of his, a buddy from the old neighborhood named Paul Marano who had become a stockbroker at Bull, Banks, Forbes & Trotsky. Paul worked in the same branch office as Lenny, Gil, and Dale, but unlike them he was neither a shark nor a barracuda. Paul Marano was a relatively honest broker as brokers go, primarily because he had inherited some family money and did not have to clean people's bones to make a living.

"I've got a problem," Joe said to Paul one sunny afternoon after they had reminisced for a while.

"What's up?"

"Can—can you keep a secret?"

"You know me, Joe. What's the problem?" Father Confessor and shrink all in one. Every broker relishes the role.

"I've got a few dollars stashed away. Money I can't show, if you know what I mean."

"How much?"

"Almost a hundred and fifty grand."

Paul whistled long and loud. This was a problem? Problems like this everyone should have.

"I'm in a cash business and—"

"Stop!" Paul held up his hand and silenced his old friend, his old neighborhood buddy. "Don't tell me any more. All I know is you've got some money you want to invest and you'd like to pay your bills in cash. Am I right?"

"That's about the size of it."

This situation was not unusual. Most brokers have a few cash customers on their books, and the best policy with them is not to ask too many questions; it is better not to know too much. What you don't know you don't have to report to the authorities: where the money comes from, who's using a phony name or his dead brother's social security number. The SEC requires brokers to "know their clients," in a financial sense that is. But there are times when knowing too much can be bad for business and even dangerous to your health.

"Here's how it works," Paul continued. "If a client pays a bill for $10,000 or more in cash, banks and brokerage houses are supposed to notify the feds. Actually, anything suspicious is supposed to be reported. So what you want to do is bring your money out $8,000 and $9,000 at a time and put it where it doesn't show, unregistered tax-free bonds mostly. Maybe some stocks with tax-deferred dividends you don't have to report."

"So what do you think?"

"For starters let's get you ten municipal bonds selling at a discount to keep the bill under ten grand. We'll ship the bonds out to you in bearer form. You put them in your box and clip coupons twice a year to collect your interest. Simple and safe."

"And nobody will know about it?"

"No way. It's the accepted way to launder money. Hell, if the federal government ever investigated the tax-free bond market, half the politicians would wind up in jail for tax evasion."

"You—you don't think what I'm doing is wrong?" Joe Ferguson revealed his guilt for the first time.

"Wrong! Look at it this way: it's the way the system works. Taxes are too high and everybody's looking for a way to beat them. The federal government even helps people out by creating loopholes like tax-free bonds and shelters. They make it *legal* to steal money from *them*. Besides, it's not wrong to steal from a thief and the federal government is the biggest crook in the country. No, I don't think what you're doing is wrong. If BBF&T paid me in cash under the table each week I'd do the same thing you're doing."

So Joe Ferguson bought municipal bonds for the first time in his life, and a week later he returned to pay for them with his trouser and shirt pockets stuffed with bills. One by one he took them out, wrinkled twenties and fifties reeking of beer and booze, and started to drop them on Paul's desk. Marano turned blue and pushed them away as though they were tainted with the plague.

"Good Christ almighty! Don't give them to me! They'll think I'm running a bookie operation here. Throwing cash on a broker's desk. Oh, my God!"

Paul led Joe to the cashier's window, where he counted out $8,845.75 and passed it across the counter. The clerk took the wad, counted it himself, and issued a receipt without batting an eyelash.

A month later they repeated the transaction, and three weeks after that Paul sold Joe $9,000 worth of utility stock with tax-deferred dividends. They spaced the trades three or four weeks apart, and by the fall of 1977 Joe Ferguson had about $140,000 invested primarily in municipal bonds, treasury bonds, tax-deferred utilities, with a few blue chips thrown in for diversity. After all, there was nothing unusual about a man earning $25,000 a year having a brokerage account showing $60,000 worth of stocks.

Everything went smoothly until the summer of 1978. A subtle change took place in Joe Ferguson and his friend and broker, Paul Marano, was quick to notice it.

"Everything okay?" he asked Ferguson over the phone.

"Oh, I don't know. My wife's giving me a hard time lately."

"What's wrong?"

"She figures what we're doing is—isn't right somehow. Like maybe there's something wrong with it."

"What the hell, Joe. I explained to you a while ago, it's the *only* way. There's no other way to do it, believe me."

"She thinks maybe we should just stick the money in the bank. Aboveboard, you know what I mean?"

"In the bank! Are you crazy? You can't just push a wheelbarrow full of money in the bank and deposit a hundred and fifty grand just like that. You'd have IRS on your back before you got out the door."

"I know, I know. I told her all that. But she still don't feel right. She gets migraine headaches all the time now."

"For Christ's sake. Nothing worse than an Irish Catholic conscience. Tell her to make a novena and forget about it, will you?"

"If she knew this was the end of it, it'd be okay. But there's more."

"More?"

"More money."

"How—how much?"

"Oh . . . another fifty grand or so. Maybe more."

"Holy shit! You've really got problems, don't you? Ever think of packing it in and retiring in Mexico or someplace cheap?"

"What do you think? What should I do?"

"Same thing. I'll get you ten bonds today and you—"

"I been thinking, Paul."

"What about?" Marano could smell trouble wafting through the receiver.

"What do you think of these gambling stocks?"

Marano sensed this was coming. He could *feel* it building a month ago.

"Forget it. They're not for you."

"Jesus, Paul, I don't know. I heard about a couple of guys making a bundle on them."

"You've already got a bundle, two bundles even. You're very well off, Joe. You don't need to make another killing. Concentrate on preserving what you've got now."

"Fuck it, Paul. Easy come, easy go. I don't mind taking a chance."

"Bullshit! You work seventy hours a week for your money. You *earn* it. You're not a racketeer or a murderer. You're entitled to it, for Christ's sake. Stop feeling guilty, will you?"

"How much is Bally?"

"Too much, God damn it."

"I won't go in big. Just a small shot, okay? How much is it?"

"Forty-two dollars a share."

"Buy me 100. Make it 200. That comes to about $8,500, right? I can afford to take a shot."

"Okay, pal, 200 Bally at the market. This is your idea, remember that."

"Look, Paul. I'm taking a shot with eight grand, that's all. If I lose it, it's my problem, right? I'm not a crybaby. I won't blame anybody but myself."

A week later Bally pushed ahead to 50. The gambling stocks and gambling-related issues were hitting new highs every day. Until this point Joe Ferguson and Paul Marano had spoken on the phone once a week or so. Now Joe was on the phone two or three times a day to get quotes on Bally.

"Jesus, Joe. You're getting as bad as some of my other clients. Take it easy, will you? You used to be a nice, easygoing guy. All of a sudden you're starting to stutter and twitch your mouth when you talk."

"Wh—what do you thing of Caesar's World, Paul?"

"It's under investigation now. The New Jersey gaming commission thinks the board of directors is straight out of *The Godfather*. Forget it."

"H—how much is it?"

"Thirty-two and a half."

"Maybe I should pick up a couple of hundred shares. What do you think?"

"I think you're crazy. Why don't you take an extended vacation to Hawaii? Take your wife on a trip around the world. Relax a little."

"Buy me 300 Caesar's World. That's only nine grand or so. I'll bring the money in tomorrow."

Two weeks passed and Bally was up to 60 and Caesar's World hit 48. Joe Ferguson came in unexpectedly one morning at 9 A.M. sharp, while Paul Marano was still engrossed in his newspaper and sipping his morning coffee. Joe was smiling wickedly. He was carrying a briefcase, which he placed on Marano's desk. He lit up a cigarette and Marano noticed his fingers were stained a dark yellow-brown from nicotine. His eyes were red-rimmed and he stuttered more and more when he talked.

"I never knew you smoked, Joe."

"Just started. I quit drinking a month ago and took up cigarettes. I don't know why. I need them, I guess."

"Why don't you quit them and start drinking again? You had it right the first time. What have you got there?"

Ferguson opened his briefcase and pulled out a thick batch of certificates wrapped tightly in rubber bands. "I'm bringing these back," he said, twitching his nose and mouth spastically.

"Bringing them back?"

"All these stocks and bonds you sold me. They're all here."

"You—you mean you want me to keep them here for you in Street name?"

"I—I'm bringing them back. I don't want them anymore. My wife can't sleep at night. She has backaches and migraine headaches. Where's your ashtray?"

"So what do you want me to do with them?" Marano had never seen his friend looking so disheveled. Ordinarily a dapper man with starched shirts and combed hair, Ferguson looked as though he were coming off a four-day bender in one of his own gin mills. He hadn't shaved in two or three days, his eyes were red and wild, and his clothing was wrinkled and stained with old booze and roast beef juice.

"I want to sell them. I—I don't want them anymore."

Marano checked the certificates and noticed that the coupons had never been clipped on any of the municipal bonds.

"You never clipped the coupons for your interest," Paul said, bewildered. "How come?"

"I never bothered, Paul. I just put them in the box and left them there. I never needed the money or anything, you know."

"I see. Well, uh, you want me to sell everything you have here, right? Everything I bought for you in the past two years."

"Everything except the gambling stocks. Sell everything and put the money in Bally and Caesar's World. All right?"

"You've thought about this all very carefully? You discussed it with your wife and decided you want to sell all your tax-free bonds, all your utilities and blue chips, and shoot the whole fucking works on the crap table? Is that right?" Marano's voice tottered on the precipice of quiet, barely concealed hysteria. Anybody else he would have been happy to accommodate and rack up hefty commissions for himself, but Joe Ferguson was an old friend. Family almost.

"This is my big shot," Ferguson said, avoiding Marano's

eyes. "If I lose, I lose. It's as simple as that. My wife's behind me on this. We decided to shoot the works and see if we can run it up to a million. If we pull it off I'm going to retire young and get out of the rat race. My wife can't take it anymore. All the hours, all the scheming to put away a nest egg. Fuck it! This is it. A million bucks and we'll buy a house down on the Jersey shore next to all the Irish judges and politicians and never worry about anything again for the rest of our lives."

Marano studied his friend closely. It was hopeless; he really meant it. He would never admit it openly. He probably did not understand fully the torment that was gripping him. But he was determined to blow everything in the market. He was determined to give it all back, every nickel he had stashed away all these years. It was a combination of greed and guilt. Joe Ferguson had gone one step beyond the fear-greed syndrome. Fear had brought him to Paul Marano in the first place. Greed replaced fear in the midst of the gambling craze when so many people were making thousands of dollars every day, on paper at least. Finally, guilt had taken over and would cause him to lose everything, to give it all back. Deep inside, Joe Ferguson did not believe that he deserved all his money. On the surface he convinced himself that he would quit if only he could parlay his stake into a million dollars. In reality, there was no way he was ready to handle being a millionaire. If he rode his small fortune up to a million, neither he nor his wife would be able to live comfortably with themselves. They would not rest until they had done their penance, paid their dues, wiped themselves clean and gone back to being hardworking, God-fearing, middle-class Americans again.

"Paul."

"What is it, Joe?"

"I read somewhere about buying stocks on margin. What do you think? Maybe I should do it all on margin. All right?"

Joe Ferguson is still trying desperately to wipe himself out completely. He kept on buying Caesar's World all the way up to 62 and Bally as high as 65. Caesar's World split 3 for 2 in November, 1978, and then the market collapsed. The split shares fell back into the teens and Bally tumbled with them. He had a paper loss of well over 50 percent by January, 1979. Paul Marano managed to talk him out of going on margin so Ferguson is still worth somewhere around $80,000. Otherwise, his position and his money would have been all but obliterated.

Ferguson will probably never forgive his old friend for keeping him relatively solvent. At this writing he is still searching frantically for new ways of losing all his money.

"What do you think of Network One?"

"A dog. A disaster. Stay away from it."

"I think I'll buy 1,000 shares. It's just a shot. If I lose, I lose. You know what I mean?"

"I know what you mean."

"Do you know anything about King International?"

"Avoid it like the plague. Nobody knows anything at all about these outfits."

"Pick me up 500 shares. What the hell? Easy come, easy go. You only live once, right?"

Joe Ferguson is much happier these days. He is clean-shaven once again and the red eyes and twitches are gone. He went to Smokenders and quit the weed completely, and he is back up to half a quart of scotch a day again. Whatever he steals from IRS he plows into every piece of garbage he hears about from every drunk he meets who never had $20 in his life—$8,000, $12,000, $15,000 at a time.

"If IRS wants to call me in, fuck it. We only go around once in this world. You might as well enjoy yourself and take the consequences. We all pay the piper sooner or later, right?"

"Right, Joe."

"It all comes out even in the end, right?"

"Right, Joe. That's 2,000 Capone Enterprises at the market. I'll call you later with the prices."

Joe Ferguson will never be rich.* He'll never make his million and retire on the Jersey shore with all the Irish politicians and judges. But what the hell? He's happy again. He can sleep at night now and his wife's migraines are gone. No more tax-free bonds burning a hole in his safe-deposit box. No dividend checks coming in every few months from the utilities, reminding him of his hidden money and stoking up the guilt.

From now on it's buy 1,000 of this and sell 1,000 of that. From now on it's quick trading in the market, never knowing at any given moment how much his portfolio of X-rated stocks is worth, how much he made or lost last week. From now on it's easy come, easy go, make a million or lose it. From now on it's all aboveboard, out in the open, a public record for anyone to see. Joe Ferguson has nothing to hide. He's a hardworking citizen. He pays his dues and keeps his slate clean. When he dies it will be with a clean conscience. No hiding in safe-deposit boxes for him.

* In the spring of 1979 the gambling stocks rallied again and Ferguson was up over $50,000. The luck of the Irish was with him and he seemed destined to make a bundle despite his best efforts to lose everything he had. At this point he insisted on going on margin. This way, the next time the market crashed, he would be sure to see his fortunes obliterated along with the rest of the plungers.

CHAPTER FIVE

Searching for the System

AT THIS MOMENT IN AMERICA at least 100,000 citizens are looking for a way to beat the market. They are all looking for a system that works. *The* system. Newcomers to the market and grizzled old veterans alike are convinced there is a system, a method of playing the stock market that is better than all others. They are convinced that somewhere down there in the canyons of Wall Street, or in the corporate heartland of America, somebody knows something they don't know. Somebody *knows*. All they have to do to beat the market is find the ones who know and follow them.

Consequently, the searchers after the secret system are always trying to unearth the True Insiders. Who are they and what are they saying? These investors devour *The Wall Street Journal* every day, and find it hard to breathe if they spend a weekend without *Barron's*.

Especially *Barron's*. *Barron's* is the place where all the wizards and financial gurus advertise their services to the public.

Let's assume you are searching for *the* market system. You read *The Wall Street Journal* and the financial pages of *The New York Times* every day, and this daily experience leaves you with a faint uneasiness. There is a hint that something is going on there between the lines but you can't quite put your finger on it. You are convinced there is a bundle to be made in the market if only you can unlock the message between the lines, if only you can decode the hidden meaning behind the words.

There are secrets to be obtained from both the *Journal* and the *Times,* but deep down in your heart of hearts you know that the real key to beating the market is contained somewhere in the pages of *Barron's.* On Sunday morning you run down to the local store for hot bagels or bread, the Sunday *Times,* and the latest issue of *Barron's,* which is hot off the presses, the ink still steaming on the page.

And what do you find in *Barron's?* After skimming Alan Abelson, you turn the page and find yourself besieged by one clamoring advertisement after another, all of them competing for your undivided attention. Dines and Holt are there, of course, and Zweig and some of the better-known market mavens. Interspersed with them are a couple of dozen additional ads worthy of the pages of the *National Enquirer.* The headlines shriek: Are Your Best Stocks in BIG DANGER? Stock Selections THAT WORK! All New Daily Graphs with 20 NEW EXCITING FEATURES. AND MORE! 101 WINNING TRADES OUT OF 142 (71.1% CORRECT!). Warning: MARKET TO CRASH . . . KILLERWAVE ACTIVITY! Telephone HOT-LINE on Our Stock Selections. Our System Is a PROVEN WINNER. It's Not Too Late to GET AHEAD. To Those Who Love to GAMBLE AND WIN. Now Is the Time to Get Ready for THE COMING DEFLATION! Join the Winning Team with Our WINNING SYSTEM. GOLD! SILVER! CRASH! BOOM!

Your head is spinning. Somebody *knows.* Somebody is making a fortune out there. But which one do you listen to? Which market letter do you subscribe to? The Bulls, the Bears, the In-betweens, they can't all be right. What are you going to do?

What you end up doing is what you always end up doing when you read the money magazines: you start clipping coupons. $10 for this trial subscription; $7.50 for a free issue PLUS an exciting new booklet called *83 Ways to Make $16,000,000 in a Flat Market;* $5 for TWO free issues, only $345 if you want to subscribe for a whole year. SAVE now! FREE! BONUS! You CAN'T AFFORD to pass this by!

During the next two or three weeks your mailbox is crammed with fourteen trial market letters, eight booklets, and six full-length books. Your mailman is threatening to lie down and kick his feet if you don't slip him a few bucks on the side to deliver all this merchandise. He wants to start charging you by the pound. This search of yours is costing you MONEY, but what the hell, it's worth springing for three or four hundred bucks if it will lead you to the right system. A $300 investment now can make you a million later. Just one BIG HIT, that's all you want. You're not greedy. Take your money and retire early. Live like a civilized human being. Forget this rat race forever.

You start reading the literature and you're suddenly more confused than you were before. One guru is predicting a crash while the next one is telling you to load up on stocks now for the breakout ahead. Go short, go long, buy puts, sell calls, write covered, write naked, buy gold, sell silver, buy francs, sell dollars, move to Switzerland, sell your house, buy another house, buy a shotgun and move to a cave, sell your cave and put your money in soybeans.

It's enough to give you a headache.

Where do you start, whom do you listen to? Somebody *knows* but who is it? The contradictions, the double-talk, all this countervailing advice is driving you crazy. You decide to follow two or three suggestions on paper, just to see how good some of these experts are.

Buy RCA at 25. You follow RCA for nine days straight. RCA goes from 25 to 30, then falls back to 26. God damn it! You could have made a fast $500 on 100 shares of RCA, assuming you had gotten out in time. But this expert forgot to tell you when to sell it. You need somebody who tells you when to sell as well as when to buy.

Expert number two recommends gold at $250 an ounce. Within a week gold forges ahead to $260, then slips back to $220. Keep buying gold, the expert says. It'll hit $300 by June, and $400 by the next lunar eclipse. For Christ's sake! If you wait long enough you'll also be old and gray before you turn a profit.

Guru number three is a newcomer called Thor Borealis. He uses astrology to plot the market, and he's looking for an explosion sometime within the next few weeks. Look for the Dow to run up 100 points or so. You sit tight and hold your breath. Sure enough, the market explodes exactly when he said it would and Ecological Industries, a small over-the-counter stock he recommended, makes a quick run of 15 points.

My God! You've found him. He *knows*. He called the turn exactly right and he even pinpointed a winning stock. The analysts at BBF&T and all the other brokerage houses missed the boat completely. The institutions were left on the sidelines with their cash in hand. Only Thor Borealis saw the blast-off coming. You dash off a check for $70 and send in for a six-month subscription to his letter. Next time you're going to be in on the action.

Thor Borealis makes his next prediction: Mars is in conjunction with Pluto. Afghanistan is going to invade Iran and the market is going to soar to 1300. BUY OF THE WEEK: Seaweed Enterprises at 3½−4 a share. Look for 17 within three weeks when the moon will be in Scorpio and the market will tumble.

This is it. Time to take a plunge and make a hit. You call your broker at Bull, Banks, Forbes & Trotsky.

"Hi, Gil. How've you been?"

"Hello, there. Where've you been keeping yourself?" Gil Clark hasn't spent five seconds on the phone with you in the past six months. The last time you called him to complain about an undecipherable monthly statement, he put you on hold for forty-two minutes. His secretary eventually cut you off and you hung up in disgust.

"What can I do for you?" he asks cautiously, ready to press the hold button if you are not calling to do some business.

"What do you know about Seaweed Enterprises?"

Gil never heard of the bloody stock. Madly he thumbs through his Standard & Poor's book while intoning gravely into the phone, "Very interesting situation . . . extremely interesting. What do *you* hear about it?"

You tell him about this great new stock maven you've found and his previous track record. You are a bit too embarrassed to tell him, however, about Borealis's eccentric approach to market forecasting.

"Claims the stock can go to 17 in three weeks," you say.

Meanwhile, Gil locates Seaweed Enterprises in his S&P guide. Thinly traded OTC company, small float with insiders holding 70 percent of the existing stock. Shows a deficit for the past five years, but is expected to earn 7 cents a share next year. A real piece of shit, which is way overpriced at $3 a share. To you Gil says,

"Could be a very exciting turnaround situation. Possible takeover candidate. A real sleeper. Definitely worth a shot."

"You're sure?"

"Sure! Look, there's always an element of risk in these situations. On the other hand, it could turn out to be a real mover. It's up to you."

"Buy me 1,000 shares."

"Done! A thousand at the market. I'll get back to you later."

You've finally found a winner. Thor Borealis is somebody who *knows,* and his recommendation has been seconded by your broker. How can you go wrong? You've already added up the numbers—1,000 shares at 3½, maybe 3¾. That's less than four grand. You'll play it smart and sell the stock at 11 or 12—well, maybe 13 or 14. No point trying to squeeze the last point and get caught holding the bag. That's 1,000 shares at 14 for $14,000, a profit of $10,000 in three weeks. You're on your way.

Gil buys your stock and logs the entry into his book. Son of a bitch, he says to himself. It's about time he gave me some business instead of complaining about his goddamn statement every month. Then Gil gets ready to do some more business.

He makes a list of his twenty biggest suckers and starts dialing and smiling.

"Hi, Herb. Gil here. Look, I'm onto something very hot. I want you to buy 1,000 shares of Seaweed Enterprises. Could be a doubler in a week or so."

He makes a mental note to get everybody out between 5 and 6 if the tip works out. Everybody except you, that is. You're the shnook who put him onto this piece of garbage in the first place. You're on your own.

Sure enough, the publicity in Borealis's newsletter and sudden buying activity push the stock up to 6 on rising volume in a week and a half. You're beside yourself with glee. This time you're in like Flynn. You're flying home. You can't lose now. And then, as quickly as it started, the stock begins to fall apart. The massive breakout Borealis predicted never materialized. The overall market, as a matter of fact, resembles the French army in full retreat from Moscow. Seaweed Enterprises is falling like a rock, a victim of heavy selling pressure which is generated to a great extent by Gil Clark leading his other clients toward the exit. It finally crash-lands at 1¼ bid, 1¾ asked, and lies there like a sick dog.

You are furious now. Borealis turned out to be another financial guru with feet of clay (or, more likely, another crook on the take for pushing stocks some manipulators want to run up a few points and then unload). And your broker! Your own broker backed him up on it. You call Gil first thing in the morning.

"Gil Clark here."

"What happened to my stock?" you scream.

"Stock? You mean Seaweed Enterprises? You tell me. You're the one who found it."

"But you—you checked it out! You said it was a turnaround situation, a takeover candidate. You—"

"Can you hold on a minute, please? I've got long distance on my other line."

Click, you're on hold. You'll die on hold if you don't hang up and stop looking for gurus.

You decide that market letters are not the answer. All these experts establish a reputation by calling the turn on one or two stocks, they attract a following as a result, and then the pressure on them mounts. They must come up with new ideas that work in order to retain their clientele. They are expected to pick winner after winner to satisfy the insatiable demands of greedy investors. Never mind that they picked a stock which tripled six months ago. What have they done lately? The market mavens are only as good as their last prediction. One or two mistakes in a row and the public retreats from them in droves as though they had just come down with a contagious disease. People look for more consistent clairvoyants. Most of the gurus eventually burn themselves out. Their luck deserts them, they run out of ideas, sources of information are not always reliable, and their track records fall apart.

At this point in your search you decide to keep your own charts. Charting is the answer. Technical analysis. The price movements of a stock hold the key to the future. Head and shoulder tops, double bottoms, resistance and support levels. Forget about the fundamentals. You don't need to know if all the workers in America are going to walk off the job tomorrow morning, or if the President has just declared war on Sardinia. In fact, you don't *want* to know. All these extraneous details are mere distractions. You've heard the stories making the rounds on Wall Street, the one about the famous chartist who worked in a windowless room so he could not be distracted by the real world, and the other story about a technical analyst who saved his *Wall Street Journal*s for three weeks before he read them because he didn't want to be influenced by current events.

You don't have to know what's going on since the charts tell it all. Breaking news is already discounted in the price movements of a stock before the news is made public. The patterns on the page are better than a crystal ball. They tell you what the *insiders* are doing beforehand, in anticipation of all the fundamentals. If U.S. Steel plummets to $6 a share for no apparent reason, you can be damned sure that World War III will be announced next week sometime. Those in the know are aware of it ahead of time.

If ever a system was designed for those susceptible to the conspiracy theory of history, it is technical analysis. The wonder of it all is that this arcane, bizarre craft is still taken seriously by most of the major firms on Wall Street. Someday soon, one hopes, the chartists will be relegated to the same level in purgatory currently occupied by the alchemists of yesteryear. It is a fate long overdue. In the meantime, such reputable pillars of the financial world as Bull, Banks, Forbes & Trotsky maintain $100,000-a-year positions on their staff for practitioners of this exotic pseudoscience.

The thing that lends an element of credibility to charting as a method of predicting the future is the fact that there is a kernel of truth present. The measure of truth is about equal to that inherent in the theory that the Trilateral Commission rules the world, or that the Rockefeller interests engineered the war in Vietnam for financial gain. Yes, there is some truth to all these claims, but it is hardly enough on which to base a major school of investment analysis.

It is also true that certain stocks will start to move down immediately prior to the release of bad news on the company, and vice versa. Obviously, someone is acting on this news before it is made available to the public. *Insiders* are getting a jump on the rest of us.

Is this true?

Look at it this way. Senior executives of major corporations are privy to information about their corporations before anyone else is. Since they are close to the decision-makers (and may even be among them), they know before the news is announced that their company is going to cut the dividend on its common stock or, conversely, that it is about to be absorbed by some giant conglomerate. News of this nature usually has a dramatic effect on the price of a stock, so they stand to make a bundle if only they can act immediately. But they are restricted by the SEC, which forbids insiders to trade on information before it is released to the public. If they simply short 1,000 shares of XYZ before a sizable dividend cut is announced, they are subjecting themselves to a hefty fine and can even end up behind bars. If they know there will be a tender offer for their company's stock at $40 a share and it is currently selling at 20, they can load up on the stock and ride it up to 35 before unloading with a $15-a-share profit. This type of trading is illegal.

In reality, however, a good deal of insider activity does take place. Accounts can be opened in someone else's name so the trades cannot be traced back to the insider. And many wealthy people with access to this type of information maintain foreign bank accounts, primarily in Switzerland, where stocks can be traded in secrecy without the SEC or IRS ever becoming aware of it. Needless to say, capital gains and other taxes are also avoided in this fashion.

But even true insiders get burned from time to time. Swiss bankers maintain that only about 65 to 70 percent of these trades turn a profit for the insider. In many instances the corporate schemers overestimate the impact of breaking news on their companies' stocks, or they make other mistakes in judgment. So we see that even in these cases, with the best type of inside information available, the success rate is less than ideal. Better odds than most of us face, but short of foolproof nonetheless.

What all this boils down to is, yes, price movements on a chart *can* tell us something before the fundamentals do. Sudden squiggles downward or upward on unusually high volume often presage breaking news, which does not hit the newspapers until a few days or a week later. Something is *happening*. Somebody is either dumping large blocks of stock or taking a huge position for a reason.

The problem is, patterns on a chart are just as much a crapshoot in predicting long-term trends as throwing darts at random. Chartists are best at calling sudden movements upward or downward for the short term. If a stock sits at 25 for three months on an average volume of 6,000 shares a day and it suddenly drops 2 points on rising volume, the chartists interpret this as a sign that the stock will fall even further. They immediately start searching in their charts for previous support levels.

Ah! They've found it. The word goes out to all the brokers in their firm that the downside risk on the stock is now 18. Look for the stock to firm up there. This could be a place to start accumulating it again. *On the other hand* (every other sentence in an analyst's report begins with *on the other hand*), if the stock penetrates through 18 with any conviction, look for further weakness in it all the way down to its *previous* previous support level of 13. *On the other hand,* if the stock indeed does bottom out at 18 and makes a U-shaped pattern, you can look for an upside ride to the 24–26 range again. Accumulate at 19 or 20 on the way back up and start selling at 24. *On the other hand,* the stock could pull back again at 21, a secondary resistance level, so be prepared to cut your losses at 16 if the stock comes down with the bubonic plague.

The trouble with all this twaddle is that it tells us absolutely nothing other than the fact that heavy buying or selling has occurred at certain price levels in the past. Technical analysis pretends to see certain trends in the price movements of stocks based on past performance; in reality it is little more than sophisticated fortune-telling dressed up with impenetrable Street jargon and fancy graphs. It is even less honest than the fortune-telling of gypsies since it is replete with qualifications and self-compromising gibberish.

In the vast majority of cases, the strong buy or sell signals on stocks are given relatively late in the game by chartists with the major firms. A stock like Polaroid will move from 23 to 40, for example, before an analyst with a prestigious outfit like BBF&T decides to recommend it. At this point the stock has built up such a head of steam that it takes another 10 points at least to slow the damned thing down. A company like Perkin-Elmer, which was a great buy for such a long time between 16 and 18, had a sell on it and did not become a strong buy recommendation until it bulled its way up to 30. When you follow the chartists you can usually be sure you are getting in on the final stages of a move. You'd better be prepared to take a quick profit and run like a thief because the *sell signal* on the stock won't occur until it has plummeted 30 percent below your purchase price in a rapidly expiring market.

Why is this so? Why is it that intelligent men and women with doctorates and MBA's and a quick grasp of numbers are so hesitant about committing themselves? Why is it that these pinstriped denizens of the point-and-figure chart are so guarded in their projections that it is often difficult to tell whether they are saying buy or sell?

The reason has to be that there is too much to lose if they are crashingly wrong. These are high-priced quick-sketch artists we are talking about here. Where else can somebody who knows how to draw lines on a graph earn $60,000 to $100,000 a year for his or her labor? The market is limited for skills such as these, skills which can easily be acquired by a bright eight-year-old with a touch of duplicity in his heart. Therefore, the rules of survival dictate a certain caution in one's prognostications. A chartist who wants to keep his job needs to develop a nimbleness of foot. You don't want to get pinned against the wall with an obvious clunker. Neither can you afford to be too bearish since you are working in an industry which depends for its livelihood on people buying stocks with great regularity. If you want to be a chartist and last, you had better learn to dance, to bob and weave, to slide with the punches. You had better give yourself an "on the other hand" or two to save your skin when the market turns against you.

There are too many whiz kids out there with their pencils and their graphs panting for your job.

* * *

"Lenny, what does your man downtown think about the market?"

"He's looking for 1300 on the Dow by next August. We moved up 20 points this week so far on rising volume. If we push through 850 with any conviction, we'll start the third leg of the secondary bull market that started a year ago. If that happens look for a major breakout of 400 points or so. The tertiary stocks should lead the way this time, along with a handful of over-the-counter issues."

"No kidding?"

"I was on the phone with my technical man just this morning. His views should be in Metz's column tomorrow."

"So what do you think?"

"Buy Seaweed Enterprises at 4. It's going to the moon."

"You're sure?"

"Sure?" Lenny covers the receiver and yells over to Gil. "You're sure about this goddamn Seaweed Enterprises, Gil?"

"Would I shit you on a thing like this?"

"Sure!" Lenny yells back into the phone.

"Okay, okay. I just want to be careful. Pick me up 1,000 shares."

"Done! A thousand at the market. I'll call you later with the confirmation."

CHAPTER SIX

Let's Hear It for the Tipsters

The newsletters are unreliable and the analysts are too slow. The only way to beat the market, you know now, is to find out what the insiders are doing. Get in on the ground floor with the smart money and make a killing before anyone else knows what's going on.

There is only one problem with this kind of approach: the number of investors who are in direct contact with genuine insiders is exceedingly small. When was the last time you were out to dinner with the chairman of the board of U.S. Steel or even a senior vice-president of Westinghouse, for example?

Consequently, the vast majority of us have to rely on hearsay for our so-called inside information. Rumors and tips. By the time a tip has been passed along to the average investor, you can be sure it has been filtered down through fourteen levels of influence at least. Remember the old party game that used to be played back in the late fifties and early sixties? Fourteen or fifteen people would line up in a row. The person at the head of the line would whisper a made-up story to number two in line—Jimmy Carter was having a secret affair with Bella Abzug twice a week at Camp David. Number two would whisper this to number three, and so on all the way down to the last individual in line. The last one to get it would write down what he had heard, and this would be compared to the original. The unintentional distortions along the way were absolutely mind-boggling. The end result might be something as bizarre as: David Susskind and Bela Lugosi were lovers for two years in Davis Park. People just can't get a story straight. Human memory is tricky and self-serving at best.

The same principle applies to stock tips. An executive of RCA makes an offhand remark about his company at a dinner party one night after his fourth martini. His comments are overheard by someone who is in the process of ordering his fifth bourbon sour, and he passes it on to his sister-in-law at her niece's wedding. The sister-in-law tells her lover, who is a partner in a law firm, and he calls his broker at BBF&T.

"Hi, Paul. Ralph here. I want you to buy me 500 RCA at the market."

Now Paul Marano knows that Ralph is a buyer of municipal bonds and tax shelters exclusively. He's told Paul on several occasions that he wouldn't touch a common stock with a ten-foot pole. For Ralph to suddenly sink fifteen grand into RCA is totally out of character. Paul writes up the order and plunks it down the tube before Ralph can change his mind, and then he tries to draw him out.

"Changed your mind about the stock market, I see."

"Not really, Paul. Something's going on over there and I figured I'd take a shot."

"Oh?"

"Keep this to yourself, Paul, but I've got it from an *absolutely impeccable* source. Seems that RCA is . . ."

Telling a broker to keep a stock tip to himself is like giving heroin to a pusher and telling him to keep it in his closet. You might as well go out and distribute it in the streets yourself. Paul doesn't even bother to return the receiver to its cradle when Ralph rings off. He's already dialing and smiling—dialing for dollars as it were—telling his top ten traders to load up on RCA. Maybe RCA will go up and maybe it won't. But ninety-nine times out of a hundred, its movement will have nothing to do with a story overheard at a party.

* * *

And then there are tips which are deliberately misleading. Sarah Raskin, who should know better since she is an ex-stockbroker herself, calls up Lenny Harris one day.

"Lenny, tell me what you know about McCulloch Oil."

"A . . . very . . . interesting . . . situation . . ." he intones while flipping rapidly through his S&P book.

"Never mind the horseshit," she replies. She knows Lenny like a book, having utilized his tricks and many he hasn't even learned yet for several years herself. "My sister knows this guy who told her to buy McCulloch. You hear anything?"

"No. How reliable is your sister and her friend?"

"He's given her two tips in the past year and they both worked out. Like a coward I sat on my hands and lost a chance to make a bundle."

"What can I tell you, Sarah? If this guy came through before, he obviously knows what he's talking about. The stock itself is a dog. If it's going to be a takeover, I don't know anything about it."

"Okay, darling. Buy me 1,000 shares. I'll take a flier."

Sarah buys 1,000 shares of McCulloch Oil at $5 a share, and within two days the stock is up to 6½ on rising volume. On the third day, without warning, the stock pulls back a full point. Volume dries up and the stock expires at 3½ bid to ⅞ asked. Sarah Raskin picks up *The Wall Street Journal* and reads a story about some Canadian operator named Kenneth Doherty, the "Canadian Diamond Jim Brady," who was arrested for stock fraud and manipulation. Among the issues in question was McCulloch Oil. Sarah calls her sister immediately.

"This guy Doherty in Canada. He—he's not your source, is he?"

"I'm afraid so, Sarah. What can I tell you? We've both been had. I'm sorry."

Sarah calls Lenny and sells her 1,000 shares at 3¼. She's down over $2,000 with commissions out in less than a week. Lenny is smiling, though. It's the best of all possible worlds for him. He made money both ways, buying and selling, and Sarah can't blame him for the debacle. Lenny rubs it in a little, just to make sure she doesn't forget whose idea this was. Sarah feels like an idiot and Lenny is in command again.

"If you *really* want to make some money," says he, "put the proceeds into Pop Shoppes. It's going to the moon."

Whatever the true insiders know they keep to themselves and a handful of very close associates. They are content to make money for themselves, and they don't want too many people getting in on the action out of fear of the SEC's becoming suspicious of any irregularity in the market.

Those who *do* go around touting stocks usually have an ulterior motive. Either they are promoters who are trying to drive the price of a stock up so they can unload a ton of it at a profit to themselves, or they are doing it out of some basic inner need. Some people need to feel important by giving the impression they are privy to secret information; others have feelings of guilt and like to feel that they are helping their fellow man; others yet have different emotional needs founded in one type of insecurity or another. Rarely does a stock tout want to do you a favor out of the goodness of his or her heart; rarely is a stock tout in a position to do so. And even in those rare situations where the motivation is pure, you can be fairly certain that the reliability of the information is questionable at best.

Perhaps one of the last people you should take a stock tip from is your broker. The broker is the last one in his firm to hear anything. Even the wire clerk in the back office gets information before the broker does.

Consider the usual sequence of events. An analyst at BBF&T writes an in-depth report on an emerging new company. The manuscript of the report is read first by his or her secretary, who types it, and then by top management (who may or may not decide to take a huge position in the stock for the firm and make a market in it). Then the report is published and disseminated through various administrative levels. Copies are sent out to the branch offices, where they are collated in the back room, and distributed by a clerk to the sales assistants (secretaries), who then place them in the brokers' inboxes.

Now the report on this great new situation is on the broker's desk. After letting it sit there for five hours or so, maybe as long as a day and a half, the broker decides to plow through the mounting pile of paper. He grabs a stack of literature just as it is about to topple onto the floor, tucks it inside his afternoon newspaper next to the sports section, and runs out to the john, where he can't be disturbed by a ringing telephone.

Sporadically, he peruses the pile of junk and tosses most of it in the can. Then he spots it, the in-depth write-up on this dazzling new company. *Interesting situation.* Attached to it there may even be a memo from his manager stating that the office has an allotment of 30,000 shares which the brokers are expected to "work on." In other words, forget for the moment that you like U.S. Steel or Honeywell or IBM or Niagara Mohawk. This is a *priority* item. The office has 30,000 shares of QRS Incorporated to work on (that is, unload upon the public), and the branch manager is damned if he is going to go back to top management (that is, his boss downtown) and tell him that his branch failed to move its allotment for the firm.

In other words: drop everything else and work on the stock!

In this instance, the broker can do one of two things. He can tell his manager to go to hell, I don't like QRS Inc. and I refuse to foist it on my customers, thereby incurring his manager's wrath forevermore and cutting himself off from a steady flow of leads, juicy accounts, and whatever other tidbits his manager might choose to drop in his lap, or he can do what's expected of him and work on the issue. Needless to say, it is an extremely rare and independent broker who would opt for the former course. His selflessness would have to border on insanity.

This procedure is the same whether the priority item is an underwriting the firm is engaged in, a stock the firm is making a market in, or a new product (insurance, real estate, mutual fund, whatever) the firm wants to try out on the public. The message is always the same: do it or else!

So Lenny, Gil, Paul, and the rest decide to *do it*. They pull out their book of clients and start dialing for dollars.

"You got a minute, Pete? Listen closely. I'm onto an exciting new *special situation*. Remember I told you, I hear things once in a while. Well. . . ."

Aside from this type of pressure imposed upon the registered reps—the brokers, the sales force, the cutting edge of the company without which there would be fewer people in the market and smaller profits for the firm—there are a good number of brokers who will work on stocks exclusively on their own. They zero in on one or two pet issues and call everyone they know plus dozens more people at random, putting them all heavily into these stocks. They build a huge position, 20,000 to 30,000 shares or more, on which they take their chances. If just one of these stocks works out they have built themselves a solid reputation. They have a loyal following of satisfied customers who regard them as geniuses, as brokers who *know* something.

It works like this. Every broker, particularly in the early stages of his or her career, is trying to build a business. He is trying to establish a book of well-heeled clients who trade regularly and provide him with a living. There are a number of ways of doing this.

One method is the scattershot, or shotgun, approach. A broker contacts a wide variety of prospective clients and tries to fit a product to their particular needs. This wealthy surgeon needs tax-free income so the broker sells him municipal bonds and shelters. This lawyer is looking for growth so the broker locates a handful of quality stocks with growth potential. A retired widow wants safety and income, so the broker matches her up with some utilities. What this broker is doing is setting himself up as a financial G.P. of sorts. He is really a marketing generalist, familiar with just about everything there is to know about investments, with a broad-based clientele. Over the long run, this is the most secure type of business for a broker to have. If the stock market turns sour, the G.P. still has his bond buyers to do business with. When the bond business is sluggish, he works with the stock traders and on real-estate and insurance deals. This is a relatively clean style of doing business, but it takes a long time to build. It is the slow road to becoming a successful broker.

Most brokers, however, are not quite so patient. They want to make it *now*. They really don't care about establishing long-range relationships with investors. One name on their book is the same as any other. Make Money Now is the name of the game. They don't want to know how many kids Jack Smith has, or about Tony Rizzo's marital problems. Here today, gone tomorrow. Churn and burn and move on to the next one. There are plenty of suckers out there to replace the old ones.

The quicker way for a broker to make it is to hit it big with a winning stock. Locate a small but solid company with potential and shoot the works. Put everybody into it.

"Bill, remember you told me if I hear of anything *really hot* to give you a call. Well, I'm onto something now."

"What is it?"

"Amalgamated Consolidated. Selling at 4½ a share and, from what I hear, could be 10 in three months."

"What's the story? Takeover or what?"

"I can't really get into that. I *hear* things, okay, if you understand what I mean. You'll be missing out real big if you don't go in for 1,000 shares or more."

So Bill buys 1,000 shares, and so does Dr. So-and-so and attorney What's-his-name. After two weeks of hustling, the broker owns 30,000 shares of Amalgamated Consolidated through his clientele. The stock has moved up a point and a half on the strength of his buying alone. He is also touting the stock to just about everyone he comes in contact with—other brokers, his dentist, cab drivers, elevator operators, even his shrink. If he can generate buying activity outside his own sphere of influence, the stock could be good for another two points or so. Perhaps others will notice heavy activity in the issue and start buying on their own, figuring something is going on over there at Amalgamated Consolidated. Finally, assuming the operation is successful, the broker starts unloading the stock, getting his best customers out first with hefty profits, maybe doubling their money or better. The broker is a genius and his clients are happy. He *knows* things. He has clout. They will do anything he says from this point on.

This is a lively scenario, but there is only one thing wrong with it: the broker who can pull it off is one in a thousand. Most major firms have restrictions on the kinds of stocks a broker can tout to his clients, and on the size of the position he can build. The vast majority of brokers lack the cleverness and the expertise to manipulate a market in this fashion and get away with it. They can only hope to get lucky and hit a winner by accident. For their tips they rely on other brokers (who might be trying to work their own hustle), on clients (who may have gotten the word from Thor Borealis or some other guru), or an operator smarter than themselves (such as the Canadian swindler arrested for his role in McCulloch Oil).

Lenny gets a tip from a client and passes it on to Gil who hustles it to his client who then tells her sister who tells her lover who calls his broker who tells the broker next to him who foists it on her own clients. Round and round it goes and the last one holding the bag is IT. Meanwhile the broker is trying to build a business quickly. If he is a smart broker, he gives each client the impression that he had lunch with the chairman of Amalgamated Consolidated just this afternoon. He conveys the impression that he is a smart young hotshot who *knows* things. The client, poor booby, thinks he or she is getting a hot tip straight from the horse's mouth.

Who knows? Maybe the broker will get lucky and the tip will work out. If not, so what? The broker makes money buying and selling and there is always the next tip and the next lineup of suckers. The gullibility of most investors is equaled only by their greed. Even though most stock tips turn out to be duds, there is the occasional one that works out, and that is enough to keep the rumor industry booming. There is never a shortage of tips to go around, nor a dearth of people eager to act on them.

Somewhere out there, somebody *knows*. And someday, maybe, you'll be lucky enough to find out who it is. But five will get you ten that special somebody will not be your broker at BBF&T, or any other firm for that matter. Not your broker, and not the high-priced analyst slaving away in his windowless room with the unread stack of *Wall Street Journals* at his elbow.

CHAPTER SEVEN

What Are the Big Boys Doing?

FEAR, GREED, AND A DOLLOP of guilt have brought you this far in your odyssey, and all you have to show for it is a drawerful of execution slips and a dwindling bank account. Let's see, forty-nine trades in the past two years and, oh my God, look at all those commissions! You started with thirty grand, lost about nine, and gave your broker over $8,000 in commissions. How can it be? Where is all that money coming from? It's magic. The great money machine in the sky is showering dollars on everybody but you.

You've had it. You've learned your lesson. No more hotshot brokers, no more worthless tips. All you've been getting is sizzle and precious little steak. The individual always gets suckered into the market too late, just before the institutions are getting ready to abandon it and leave him holding the bag. The institutions get the best advice while John Q. Public has to depend on tenth-hand information from con artists and stock touts.

The trick, you've finally learned, is to keep your eye on the institutions. The professional money managers, the banks, the mutual funds, the *big boys*. Find out what they're doing and act along with them. The institutions know how to make money in the market while the little guy always gets burned.

It isn't that difficult to stay abreast of what the institutions are doing. Subscribe to the publications catering to the institutional client and read the literature churned out by major brokerage firms which keep records on how their margin, cash, and institutional accounts have been doing. *The Wall Street*

Journal, The New York Times, and other newspapers also report on institutional activity from time to time—whether the banks and funds are buying or selling and even the particular securities they are trading.

There is only one thing wrong with keeping your thumb delicately poised on the pulsebeat of the institutions and acting along with them: your record is likely to be just as dismal as theirs. The truth is, the professional money managers have compiled an atrocious track record over the past dozen years or so. They have demonstrated a propensity for being wrong most of the time on a mammoth scale.

Consider what happened in the 1978 seesaw market which reveals a rather typical pattern. Without warning, the market exploded on an otherwise quiet Friday in April, a Friday as it happened when options for the period were due to expire. The volume was tremendous. The rally continued into the following week on higher and higher volume, reaching a zenith at a point well over 60 million shares.

What was the Street consensus for all this sudden activity? The experts were unanimous: only the institutions could have generated such massive buying power. Only the institutions sitting on the sidelines, loaded up to their vest pockets with cash, could have been responsible.

This became the accepted belief all through the big bull market of 1978, which only began to peter out as we entered the early days of summer. The institutions were buying. Again in August, without apparent warning, the buying panic resurfaced. The market took off on unusually high volume once more, and again the experts credited the bullish activity to those savvy institutions.

And then came September and the big blowoff that followed. Monumental selling on tremendous volume. A selling panic, the opposite side of the coin from the spring and summer rallies. Who was doing all this dumping? Why, the institutions, of course. Who else could wield that kind of clout? Who else had the muscle to move in and out of the market like a raging hurricane, leaving an army of victims in its wake? The institutions had done it again, suckering the little guy back into the market after they had run it up 100 points or so, and then jumping out as though on cue, leaving the rest of us high and dry. The little guy got shafted again.

This was an interesting scenario accepted for a while by most market losers as gospel truth. The problem is, it simply was not so. The institutions, as it turned out, were on the wrong side of the market themselves, as they usually are.

When the air had cleared and the accounts had all been tallied, institutional activity for the year was finally made available to the public. The institutions, it seems, were *net sellers* into the spring when the DJIA was below 800. They remained in a heavy cash position through the end of July and only began to accumulate stocks in August, toward the tail end of the second rally of the year. They came in late as is their unique specialty.

Who, then, triggered the massive buying spree that began in April? The revisionists went to work and rewrote the financial history of the year with a different plot. Foreign buying, it was determined, played the most significant role. All those Arabs and Europeans, themselves sitting on a veritable mountain of unwanted U.S. legal tender, decided to channel it into the American stock market. The dollar may have been dwindling in value from day to day, but the crafty foreigners knew that the U.S. economy was far from finished. They recognized good value when they saw it and, with all those blue chips lying there gasping for air, the decision to convert devalued dollars into shares of American industry was made almost spontaneously, it seemed. A tidal wave of greenbacks came flooding into the States, much of it finding its way to California real estate, and the rest inundating the barren plains of the equities market. The foreigners bought everything in sight. We had stuck them in the past with all our excess cash, and in 1978 they decided to turn it into something of value. A touch of modern-day alchemy, as it were.

Meanwhile, the institutions kept soaking up equities into the fall, and found themselves most heavily invested just as the market was about to collapse. In September, 1978, when the bottom dropped out, more than 50 percent of the major American institutions had a cash position of under 10 percent. About 30 percent had cash reserves of more than 15 percent. By the end of the year, however, the percentage of institutions with less than 10 percent of their assets tied up in cash had dropped to 30 percent while those holding more than 15 percent of assets in cash had risen to 43 percent. The institutions sold off stocks most heavily into the collapse at lower and lower prices. When the market hit bottom in December, they were still selling; they were doing just the opposite of what a smart money manager, a professional insider with his finger on the pulse of the economy, should have been doing.

The only investor with a worse track record than this is you, the average individual investor. While the institutions were buying and selling late, getting caught with their collective pants down around their knees, the average individual was later yet. The little guy came in after the institutions, and wound up liquidating positions in November and December as the market leveled out at rock bottom. And 1978 was not an exception. The record of the institutions during the past dozen years has been worse than that of the Dow and the S&P indexes in most cases; they fared no better for the most part than a portfolio of randomly selected stocks.

Not only do the money managers for the banks, insurance companies, mutual funds, and pension funds buy stocks relatively late into a bull market, they usually wind up buying the *same* stocks. If IBM happens to be a favorite of the day, you can be sure that most of the big institutions are heavily committed to IBM at the same time. If U.S. Steel is in disfavor for some reason, they are all dumping Big Steel at rapidly decreasing prices, again at the same time.

The institutions act en masse, as though responding to a

secret signal, buying and selling simultaneously in large quantity. The general public likewise acts as a group, moving in and out of the market in massive waves. As sluggish as the waves of institutional activity are, however, the comings and goings of the public are slower yet. Mass psychology is a devastating and almost totally irresistible force.

The main reason why most professional money managers act like lemmings when making decisions about the pools of money entrusted to them is that they cannot afford to be wrong *all by themselves*. They belong to the same club. They tend to dress, talk, and act alike and, worst of all, think alike. They meet for lunch in places where other professional money mavens hang out, and they drink in the same bars. This is not unusual since most people like to associate with their own kind. The problem here, however, is that since they are all swapping the same ideas back and forth they are apt to make the same decisions about the market. They are touting ideas to one another and buying and selling the same issues simultaneously.

If they are wrong, at least they are *all wrong together*. A portfolio manager for a mutual fund cannot be faulted too badly if 99 out of 100 mutual funds are down 10 percent on the year. Hell, all the other experts guessed wrong, too, so he's no worse than they are. But if he is wrong while all the others are right, then he can kiss his fancy plum of a job goodbye. If all the other institutions are buying RCA and he decides to hell with it, I don't like RCA, I like Texaco instead, then RCA runs up 8 points while Texaco catches pneumonia and heads south for the season, this genius is suddenly wrong all by himself. It's no fun being an individual marching to the beat of a different drummer when everyone else is marching to victory and you step off the edge of a cliff.

So the institutions move collectively, stumbling in and out of the market like a cowardly hydra-headed dinosaur. The only slower collective is the general public, which moves like a retarded mammoth a step or two behind the institutional dinosaur.

If you decide, in the final analysis, to do what the institutions are doing, you may wind up improving your performance a bit. But you will still come out a loser on net balance after inflation and taxes have taken their toll. All you will have done is to substitute one defeatist psychology for another.

There's gotta be a better way, you say. Somewhere out there somebody knows what's going on. Not everybody comes out a loser in the end.

Yes, some people are winning in the market. Before we talk about them, however, let's take a look at a unique and relatively new phenomenon in the investment world.

CHAPTER EIGHT

A Special Word About Women

WITHIN THE LAST DECADE or so women have begun to enter the stock market in droves, both as investors and as stockbrokers. Liberation, rising divorce rates, and the feminist movement in general have given women more authority over money than they've ever had before in the United States. Until recently women were regarded as financial illiterates, a notch or two above a bright ten-year-old when it came to handling money. Men put assets in their wives' names, mostly for tax reasons and legal considerations, but the responsibility for managing these assets belonged exclusively to the male of our species.

All this has changed. Jobs and careers previously regarded as off limits to women have suddenly opened up. Women are earning more money on their own and acquiring it as a result of separation and divorce. But most females in our society have not been properly trained to handle all this newfound wealth.

The entire subject of money has traditionally been a mystery to most women. Financial jargon is as alien as a foreign language. The investment world in general, like Monday-night football and other sporting events, has always been a male preserve. The same used to be true of politics, but this barrier has long since been overcome. The world of sports has also been explored in greater depth by women during the 1970's. This leaves money as the next frontier.

One of the more serious problems women have when dealing with money is their naïve belief that men know all about financial matters. By now we know this is simply not the case. Men have always pretended to know about money in the same way they have always pretended to know about politics and refused to discuss the subject with women. We have seen in previous chapters, however, that most investors are psychological basket cases when it comes to managing their accounts. Since most investors in the past have been men, this indictment has to fall most heavily on their shoulders. We know that fear, greed, and guilt are far more influential factors in the decision-making process than reason is. Reason and prudence are rarely exercised.

Women have been bamboozled into believing, however, that men have a special talent for managing money. Boys are prepared by their fathers to handle the family treasury while girls are directed into more "feminine" areas. This much is true, of course. Our society does categorize activities as male and female. Math and science are male and English and art are female subjects in school, for example. You can make a list yourself that would fill an entire volume. But what is left unsaid in all this nonsense is the fact that men have made a devastating botch of financial affairs. The country's economy is directed, mostly by men, with all the expertise of a horny teenager driving his father's car in pursuit of a Saturday-night hand job. Most men conduct their personal financial affairs in a reckless and self-destructive fashion. This is not to say that women can or will do the job any better. But the notion that men have a unique talent for understanding and managing money which is biologically denied to women is nothing more than myth. It is sheer unadulterated hogwash.

So here we are at the beginning of a new decade, and women are coming into the market with fistfuls of money they never had before. Brokerage firms like Bull, Banks, Forbes & Trotsky have been pressured by the federal government into hiring more women as brokers, along with more blacks and other minorities. Branch managers have been raking the countryside with a fine-tooth comb looking for women who are eager to enter the business. Each branch has to have a generous sprinkling of female stockbrokers on its staff or risk the wrath of the federal govern-ment.

The women are trained by the firm and sent down to Wall Street to pass the six-hour test administered by the New York Stock Exchange. Once they have their licenses they are given a desk, a telephone, and a secretary, the same as all the men brokers. Now it is up to them to *do some business.*

There is a vast new market out there waiting just for you, they are told. All those women, newly degreed, newly divorced, with high-paying professional jobs. The potential is enormous. All you have to do is reach out and pluck these ripe new pros-pects from the money trees. Yours for the asking. Since male brokers have always regarded women clients as nothing but trouble, pains in the neck anywhere except in bed, the field is wide open.

On the surface, this makes a lot of sense. Male brokers have always preferred to deal with other men as clients. Women required too much of an education and they were too quick to complain about trivial matters. They were "emotional," not rational, as men are. So, except for those rare women with piles of filthy lucre under their control and a grasp of how to handle it—masculine, rich, horsey women, as it were—stockbrokers did not pursue females as clients, and, in fact, went to great lengths to avoid them.

Susan Williams is typical of the type of woman who has been hired by major brokerage firms during the past few years. In her mid-twenties, attractive, with a bachelor's degree in hand from a good university in the Midwest, she arrived in New York with a strong desire to succeed as a stockbroker. She was hired at a Manhattan branch office of BBF&T where she was trained, and in the fall of 1978 she passed the test and got her license.

At her branch were two other women who had been work-ing there as brokers for nearly a year. Dolores Feldman was thirty-three years old, a native of Brooklyn and a current resi-dent of Manhattan, where she lived with her husband, an analyst

for a different firm. The other woman was Jane Dempsey, a
black woman originally from South Carolina, who was on the
verge of quitting.

"Oh, man, it's tough," she said to Susan and Dolores at
lunch one day. "I don't want to discourage you since you just
got into the business, but there's no way I can make it. Every
day I come to work I feel like crying. Being a woman is bad
enough, but being a black woman makes it almost impossible.
I'm looking around right now for another job, as *far away* from
Wall Street as I can get."

"How about you?" Susan turned to Dolores Feldman.
"You've been at it a year and you seem to be doing okay."

"I'm keeping my head above water. Holding my own, I
guess you can say."

"You've managed to acquire a fair number of clients since
you've been here."

"Look, let me be honest with you. The only reason I'm
making it is because of my husband. He sends me a lot of business through his contacts. If I had to do it on my own, forget it.
I'd have been out of here six months ago."

Susan had noticed before that most of Dolores's clients
seemed to be men. She had been puzzled by this and meant to
discuss it with her.

"Have either of you gone after the women's market?"

Dolores and Jane looked at each other and started laugh-
ing. Then Dolores said, "We shouldn't be discouraging you like
this. Try it for a while and see. You have to go through it yourself to know what we're talking about.

Susan Williams returned to her desk and embarked upon her
big campaign. She called up NOW and other feminist organiza-
tions, and got the names of influential women in and around the
city. She sent out mailings and arranged to do seminars on
financial planning at various clubs. At first she was ecstatic. The
turnouts were always large and the women were attentive as
she patiently explained the rudiments of the investment world.
After three months of this, however, she began to grow a bit

depressed. Hundreds of women had turned out for her lectures, but precious few of them became clients.

"I don't understand," she said to Dolores after work one day. "They're all so polite and enthusiastic at the seminars, but they never give me any business. Most of these women deal with *men* brokers from what I can figure out."

Dolores smiled sympathetically. "Now you're beginning to understand. It's hard to explain it unless you've experienced it yourself."

What infuriated Susan more than anything else was the fact that the women would come to her for advice and information; they asked her questions they were too ashamed to ask their brokers for fear of being thought stupid, and then they turned around and gave their brokerage business—and the commissions that went with it—to their men brokers.

"It's masochistic and self-destructive, yet I can't seem to break the pattern no matter how hard I try," Susan complained. "I service them with literature and information and the men make all the money. It's driving me crazy."

"How about male clients?" Dolores asked. "Have you had any luck with them?"

"The ones who give me any business at all think they have the right to sleep with me. One guy came in last week and bought a lousy 50 shares of Holiday Inns, less than $1,000 worth of stock, and then he got indignant when I refused to go out to dinner with him. I never saw anything like it."

"Now you're really learning the business," said Dolores. "You can either fuck for dollars or starve to death. The women's market you can forget about for the time being. As liberated as we think we are, we're still afraid to entrust our money to other women. We still want men to manage our money and take care of us. Until we break away from this kind of psychology, women stockbrokers are doomed to failure—unless, of course, they don't mind putting out to land the man's account. The sugar-daddy syndrome. Even then they only give us a small piece of their business in return for a piece of ass."

* * *

In a direct about-face from past policy, male brokers have started actively to pursue professional women as clients. The reason behind this is simple enough: it is strictly a question of economics. The women's market has grown too large to ignore. There are megabucks in women's hands just waiting to be funneled into the stock market. As much as men have disliked doing business with women in the past, the desire to earn bigger and bigger commissions is too powerful to resist. It's a matter of priorities. If all the lepers of the world were showered with legal tender tomorrow morning, you can bet your last nickel that stockbrokers would be out beating the bushes in pursuit of wealthy lepers.

For their part, women are still not confident about their money. They are not quite sure what to do with it. Traditionally, they have left the management of money to their men and turned to them for financial advice. Emotionally, many women find it comforting to deal with a man. The sexual nuances, even when they are covert, can be exciting. Money and sex have always gone together, natural mates in a cold alien world. It is difficult to break the age-old patterns. So the women brokers newly arrived in the business find it difficult to make a living. They get discouraged early in the game and drop out, usually into a more agreeable line of work.

Lenny Harris, Gil Clark, Dale Meredith Worthington, and the various sharks and barracudas at BBF&T and all the other brokerage firms have added more and more women to their lists of clients in recent years. They complain constantly about their female clients, yet they are loath to abandon this lucrative new market.

"Goddamn women clients give you nothing but trouble," Lenny remarked to Gil over drinks one afternoon.

"They're always complaining about the most trivial things," Gil commiserated. "You remember that blonde with the big knockers who came in to see me last week? She called me twice today to bitch about a lousy eighth of a point she paid for Westinghouse. Her sister paid 19, she said, so why does she have to pay 19⅛? Imagine that."

"They don't have the business experience, that's it in a nutshell," said Lenny. "They've been sheltered too long and don't know what it's like out here in the real world."

"You can tell what time of the month it is by the kinds of complaints you get. What a body, though. You see the tits on that broad when she sat down at my desk?"

"You getting any yet?"

"I'm debating whether to go after her or not. Once you fuck them you can kiss their business goodbye. I'm not sure yet what's more important, her pussy or her purse."

The type of psychology at play here is destructive to women investors. It's a vicious circle with no easy solution in sight.

Men don't want to do business with women—but neither do other women. Reluctantly, men go after their business because it is too profitable to ignore. Women prefer to give their business to men, yet they are suspicious and almost paranoid about the man's motivation. The sexes need each other but they often do business together for all the wrong reasons. Round and round it goes, endlessly self-defeating.

Can the pattern be broken? Yes, but only with a great deal of discipline. In Part Two we will discuss methods of turning a losing psychology into a winning one. We will talk about how stock-market losers, men and women both, can eventually become winners.

PART TWO

HOW YOU CAN BECOME A WINNER

CHAPTER NINE

Neurotics in Control

FEAR. GREED. GUILT. A belief in magic, in promises and fantasies. A need to feel that someone knows what's really going on. If these are the key reasons why most people lose money in the stock market, what then are the psychological traits which distinguish the winners? Do investors who make money consistently share any common, recognizable, definitive characteristics?

First of all, successful investors seem to have their neuroses under control most of the time at least. They have the same anxieties, doubts, and fears the rest of us share, but they have disciplined themselves to a point where they don't let their psyches interfere with their financial affairs. It may be that their compulsions run amok in other areas—sex, liquor, food, speed, whatever—but their money is secure.

For the most part, winning investors initiate their own trades. They *buy* stocks, bonds, and other securities; they don't have these items sold to them. As a result, their contact with their brokers is sporadic. They call their brokers when they need something and their brokers know enough not to call them unless it is urgent.

"I can tell by looking in someone's eyes whether or not he'll get pissed off if I call him up to sell him something," Lenny said to Gil at lunch one day. Gil agreed and added,

"Any client who calls his broker more than twice a month is looking for trouble. The ones who call every day asking for quotes are the worst suckers of all."

There is some exaggeration in this—some winners have the type of portfolio that requires careful monitoring—but it is true in the great majority of cases. The average individual investor doesn't need to talk to his broker more than once a month or so unless he has huge sums of money coming in every week that he wants to channel into the market—and then he isn't an average investor any longer.

Most successful investors have done a fair amount of homework before they enter the stock market. They've taken the time to read a book or two, a handful of pamphlets published by the brokerage firms for the novice investor, and they know the difference between a common and a preferred stock, a municipal bond and a corporate debenture. The brokers who will sit patiently with a "cold" investor, someone with zero knowledge, and provide an education in investments are few and far between.

Number one, brokers do not get paid for this. They work on commissions and earn a living only when they are making transactions.

Number two, most brokers do not have the knowledge themselves. They acquired it initially to pass the test, but that may have been ten years ago and long since forgotten. The average broker is frightfully ignorant about low-commission securities such as money market instruments, government agency bonds, municipal notes, etc. They can rattle off story after story about the string of listed stocks dancing across the wall in front of the boardroom, as well as any number of OTC issues they happen to be following, since stock business constitutes the bulk of most brokers' incomes. A few brokers have taken the time to learn the insurance, real estate, and options markets which also generate decent commissions, but the ones who do tend to specialize in these areas and neglect the rest of the financial universe.

Number three, even brokers with the knowledge are reluctant to assume the role of teacher since there is no guarantee that the pupil will become a valuable client. It could turn out to be so much time and effort flushed down the toilet.

Therefore, the chances of neophyte investors finding a knowledgeable broker who is patient and willing to spend some time educating them before generating any commissions are slim to say the least. Professional money managers and financial planners deal exclusively with big money, with people whose liquid assets total $100,000 or more, so unless you are lucky enough to qualify for this exclusive club you cannot go to them for assistance. In any event, the record of the professionals is pretty pathetic, as we have already seen, and does not justify the high cost of their services.

Most winners educate themselves and run their own money. In addition to reading books, pamphlets, and the financial papers, many have taken a course or two on the basics of investments. They have taken the time and trouble to attend an evening class for a few months to acquire the bare rudiments and the jargon of Wall Street. They understand the language and recognize it for what it is: technical gibberish, similar to the lingo spouted by lawyers and other professionals, designed to confuse the layman and make him think the subject is more complicated than it really is. By the time the winner is ready to commit his money to the securities market, he is well beyond the level of intimidation. He enjoys using the jargon because it makes him feel like a member of the club, but he knows it is little more than role-playing.

All this is preliminary to the big event. By the time the successful investor is ready to enter the financial arena, he *already knows what he wants from his money.* He knows what he wants his money to do for him. A desire to *make money* is not enough. Most people who walk into a brokerage firm with nothing more specific in mind than a longing to "make money" are heading for a fall. They have the word *loser* stamped across their eyeballs.

This is perhaps the key ingredient of all: the establishment of *financial goals.* Specific goals can be planned for and attained. "Making money" is as vague as wanting to be famous. Why? How? In what field? People who go through life wanting to be famous wind up spending their lives in obscurity. Investors who commit their dollars hoping to make money usually end up broke.

Fame is a by-product of work with a lofty target in sight, and success with money is likewise a by-product of a carefully thought-out financial plan with specific goals in mind.

When you call up your broker and tell him you want to make money, you are at his mercy. Lenny, Gil, Dale, or Paul can sell you anything BBF&T happens to be pushing at the moment with the promise that "it's going straight to the moon." Think of all the *money you'll make* if only you go in for 500 shares of Crapshooters Incorporated.

But when you call Lenny or Gil and tell him you want a utility with a tax-deferred dividend, or a good-quality growth stock with a yield of at least 6 percent and a P/E ratio under 10,* you are controlling the action. You've given him certain criteria and his job is to find suitable vehicles to meet them. You are using your broker's expertise to locate specific products to satisfy your goals.

This is how successful investors operate. They control the action. They set the goals. They utilize the services of their brokers rather than being used by them. They ask for advice when it is required, but they have enough knowledge themselves to evaluate the advice given and apply it to their own situation. When their brokers call them it is usually to tell them that something they were looking for is now available, or to ask them if they are in the market for a product which seems to fit their financial personality.

What separates the winners from the losers is most apparent when the market is slow.

* If a stock earns $2.50 a share and is selling for $25, its P/E or Price/ Earnings ratio is 10: Price divided by earnings = P/E ratio.

"Where have all the traders gone?" Gil asked Lenny during a particularly sluggish day. The market had been skidding sideways for over a month. Volume was mediocre. Business was horrendous and Gil was beginning to wonder how he was going to pay for a new sailboat he wanted. It was the middle of a doldrum period with no activity anywhere.

"Don't ask me," Lenny answered. "I don't think I have any traders left on my books. Nobody's buying anything except tax-free bonds right now."

"What do you think? You think we should be shorting this market now? You think it'll take off again or what?"

"I don't know. We need some major news. A big tax cut, elimination of capital-gains tax, double taxation of dividends, something."

"Another war maybe?"

"*Something.* Nothing's happening anywhere. The President's dull, Congress is boring, nothing's going on. We need a spark, something to ignite a little activity."

"It can't stay like this forever. Sooner or later this market's going to explode."

"That's for sure. It always does sooner or later. But it can't be too soon for me."

Lenny, Gil, and other brokers with a few years in the business have been through this several times before. They know the market moves in cycles, from the doldrums through a period of feverish whirlwind action, back to the doldrums again. Most have learned to be patient, to live on a leaner budget for a while, knowing that a good three months of frantic buying activity can make the entire year for them. When the buying time comes all the traders—the suckers and losers—will come running in together throwing bushels of money into the market.

"What should I buy? What looks good? Jesus Christ, did you see the move Tandy made last week? I know a guy made ten grand on Inexco in less than two weeks. This is it! This time it's for real. Straight to the moon. Make my bundle and quit. No more rat race for me."

Only a few investors have the foresight to buy stocks during the doldrums, when they are low in price. These few buy quietly, loading up on good-quality issues when the yields are highest and they can get the best value for their money. They avoid the crowds and act individually, bucking the trends and working counter to the hysterical waves of mass psychology. These are the winners and they constitute a small minority.

CHAPTER TEN

Investors Anonymous

To BECOME A successful investor requires breaking completely from the fear-greed-guilt cycle; it requires giving up a belief in magic and fantasy and learning to deal with reality; it requires learning to live within the realm of possibilities and establishing realizable goals; it requires the acceptance of a discipline, self-imposed rules and regulations, to take the place of impulsiveness and obsessive financial behavior.

Discipline. Rules. Guidelines instead of compulsion.

A difficult task, perhaps, but no more so than the effort required of a compulsive drinker who wants to quit drinking, a compulsive smoker or drug addict who wants to abandon these destructive habits. We are talking here about changing habits, about altering a psychological mind-set so that losing behavior can be transformed into that of a winner.

There is no morality at work here. If you feel you are not entitled to your money for whatever reason, then give it all away to charity. Joe Ferguson had his guilt complex about hiding money from Uncle Sam; others may have financial skeletons of their own lurking in the back of their closets. Otherwise, if you have acquired money through hard work and labor like most people and you want to see it grow and work for you instead of against you, then you must adopt certain rules to help you manage your money properly. You need a formula for action and formulas are mechanical. Formulas are logical and totally unemotional. We have to learn to divorce money from our feelings and anxieties, and subject it to a structured discipline. If we fail to do this we will just keep repeating the same mistakes over and over again.

In Part One we saw how losing investors kept coming back into the market and taking a beating after they had resolved firmly never to let it happen again. These people were sincere in their intentions. They meant what they said at the time as, no doubt, they will be serious about their convictions endlessly into the future. But they are operating out of control. Their habits are ingrained in their nature. They need a discipline, rules to govern their financial behavior, or they will never break the losing cycle.

In the chapters ahead we will discuss the rules which must be followed if you are going to become a successful investor. If you are serious about giving up the behavior which makes you a compulsive loser, these rules will show you how to do it. If you already are a winner, the following chapters will reinforce the winning habits you have adopted subconsciously. They will help you stay on the right path and avoid being sidetracked without realizing it later on.

This is a new beginning for all of us. These are original guidelines for Investors Anonymous designed to provide all of us with a winning formula for handling money constructively.

CHAPTER ELEVEN

Do Your Homework

IF YOU ARE NOT going to take the time to find out the difference between a common and a preferred stock, a subordinated debenture and a municipal bond, a mutual fund and a unit investment trust, then forget about the market. Keep your money in the bank.

Put a few thousand dollars in a day-to-day savings account, preferably one that gives you a check-writing privilege so you can earn some interest on your ready cash, and put whatever you won't be needing for a while into a time deposit and let it accumulate there through the magic of compound interest. Pay your taxes on the interest without grumbling and forget about it. If you are in a high tax bracket (all middle-class people are in high brackets today, 32 percent and higher, because of inflation), you'll lose out a bit to inflation in the long run, but at least your money will be safe. You won't have to worry about it or spend any time making financial decisions.

If, on the other hand, you are tired of seeing most of your money devoured by the federal monolith and you want it to grow in real earning power during the coming years, then you should make an effort to sit down and do a little homework. The subject of financial investments is not as complicated as it appears from the outside looking in. Once you have cut through all the jargon and doubletalk, it is really quite an orderly universe. It is a bit more complex than buying 500 shares of Amalgamated Rubbish and hoping to see it double overnight, but a tidy universe with everything in place nonetheless.

For starters, you might pick up copies of my own book, *Everything the Beginner Needs to Know to Invest Shrewdly*, and *How to Buy Stocks* by Louis Engel. These are the best available introductions to the securities markets you are apt to come across. Even if you consider yourself to be a grizzled veteran with years of experience behind you, it won't hurt to keep these books handy on your reference shelf. No matter how sophisticated you are, you still might be a bit hard pressed to define a participating cumulative preferred stock, for example, off the top of your head. My book gives easy-to-read, easy-to-find definitions for every conceivable type of security, while Engel goes into a bit more detail on how stocks are actually bought and sold.

If you have the time and the inclination, you might also sign up for a course in basic finance at a local college or adult education center. Some of these courses will teach you how to read a financial statement and a Standard & Poor's fact sheet besides providing you with the rudiments of the securities markets. This requires investing a bit more cash and time as well, which may or may not be available to you. If you have made the effort to do some reading on your own, you can get along without taking a course.

In addition to the books and courses, major brokerage firms publish tons of literature designed to educate the individual investor. Visit a nearby branch office and load up on whatever is available. You should be able to find pamphlets explaining the basics of tax-free bonds, shelters, different kinds of stocks, and a variety of other items. In my own experience I have found a lot of these handouts to be poorly written and sometimes filled with jargon by staff researchers who have forgotten how to speak and write good everyday English. Still, they are free and you should be able to make some sense of them, especially if you have read the introductory books beforehand.

All this has cost you a handful of dollars and a few hours of your time. Now you are almost ready to take on Lenny, Gil, Dale, Paul, and all the other sharks and barracudas on *your* terms, not theirs. In short time none of these hotshot brokers will be able to snow you with their sales hype any longer. They won't be able to hustle or intimidate you or bamboozle you with their esoteric jargon.

But you are still not quite ready to visit a branch of BBF&T, E. F. Hutton, Merrill Lynch, Shearson, Bache, or whatever firm is nearest you. You are not ready to sit down and talk with Lenny, Gil, or some other registered rep. There are a few more steps you have to go through first. Let's move on and discuss them one at a time.

CHAPTER TWELVE

Establish Your Goals

GOAL-SETTING IS THE KEY to success with money, as I mentioned briefly a bit earlier. What exactly do I mean when I talk about the establishment of financial goals?

Your goals should be specific and will depend a great deal on your particular circumstances. A single twenty-five-year-old with no obligation to anyone but himself or herself will have different goals from those of a sixty-five-year-old executive on the brink of retirement. Someone earning a salary of $80,000 a year is orbiting through a different galaxy than an individual trying to support a family on $15,000.

Even to be concerned about financial goals at all presumes that you have disposable money in the first place. If you have nothing in the bank and can barely pay your monthly expenses, your main goal should be to find a way to upgrade your standard of living. If your income is sufficient to pay your bills and there is enough left over to stash away and build up a substantial reserve fund, then you are ready to think about investing some of this idle cash.

The first consideration for anyone with a middle-class income or higher should be taxes. *Think taxes!* Virtually all middle-income families are in high tax brackets these days. Salaries of $25,000 to $30,000 a year today are equivalent in real buying power to a $15,000 annual income a decade ago, but they are taxed at a much higher bracket. The financial wizards in Washington have failed to index tax brackets to the true inflation rate, so we all wind up taking home less of every extra dollar we make.

In addition to tax considerations, there are a couple of other basic rules you should follow when establishing financial goals. Generally speaking, the more idle cash you have, the more conservative you should be with it; conversely, those with relatively small sums can afford to speculate or risk a larger percentage of it.

Why?

Because the income from $50,000, for example, will amount to perhaps $4,500 or $5,000 a year, enough to provide you with a few extra amenities in life. The income generated by only $10,000 is too puny to worry about. Consequently, you can afford to lose a piece of it without it affecting your life-style to any significant degree.

Let's take a look at some specific numbers now. You are in a 32 percent tax bracket or higher. You own a house or an apartment which gives you a handsome tax write-off each year as well as a chance to build up equity for the future. You are able to pay your bills each month, perhaps by utilizing a few sleight-of-hand check-balancing maneuvers, and you have a chunk of cash sitting in a bank account. What should you do with this money? What type of financial goals should you establish for yourself?

That depends, naturally enough, on how much money you have. If the amount is

$5,000   Leave your money where it is. You need a ready cash reserve, walking-around money as it were, and you'd best keep this cash as safe and liquid as possible. An alternative to a day-to-day savings account is a money-market fund, which currently pays about 10 percent interest, although this figure could decline by the time this book is published. In a money-market fund your cash is virtually as safe as it is in a bank, and just as liquid.

$10,000   Leave $5,000 in a savings account or a money-market fund.

The balance is too small to invest for income. Your main goal should be to see this $5,000 grow to a larger sum. Your goal is *growth*. You might allocate $3,000 for good-quality growth stocks and *risk* $2,000 on more speculative issues.

$20,000   Keep $5,000 in a bank or a money-market fund. $15,000 is still too small a figure to invest for income. Put $10,000 into good-quality *growth* situations, and *speculate* with the other $5,000.

$50,000   Keep $5,000 in a bank or a money-market fund. Now we can talk about *income* as a financial goal: $30,000 might be earmarked for *tax-free* or *tax-advantaged* income, $10,000 for good-quality *growth*, and the last $5,000 for *speculation*.

$75,000   Leave $5,000 in a bank or a money-market fund. Allocate $50,000 for tax-free or tax-advantaged *income*, $15,000 for good-quality *growth*, and $5,000 for speculation.

$100,000 and over   Put $5,000 to $10,000 in a bank or a money-market fund; $70,000 plus should go into tax-free or tax-advantaged *income*, $20,000 plus into *growth*, and a small percentage, 5 to 10 percent depending on your temperament, should be put at *risk*.

The above breakdown is strictly a general guideline and should not be treated as though it were written in stone. The percentage apportioned to each goal will depend on your own special circumstances, family, social, and otherwise. In *The Optimist's Guide to Making Money in the 1980's* I set up five sample portfolios for five hypothetical cases based on age, income, and family situation. After you have done some homework by reading an introductory work or two, you might turn to this book for a more detailed explanation.

The main point here is *not* that you have decided to put 30 percent into growth as opposed to 40 percent, but rather that you have established financial goals for *different pools of money*. You have divided your cash into categories and labeled each category with a financial objective. You have separated your money into *ready reserves, income, growth,* and risk or *play* money. If you are starting out with $30,000 and you know beforehand that $5,000 is earmarked for *play,* you are prepared to lose this five grand shooting crap with Lenny, Gil, or Dale, but *not a nickel more.*

This is where the discipline comes in. You have to establish the rules *before* you walk into BBF&T and ask to speak to a broker. You know ahead of time that x amount of dollars is *safe* money and y is for *play,* and you have to have the discipline to *stick to your goals.* If you lose all your y dollars taking a shot with Paul, *that's it.* No more gambling until you have found some additional y dollars to replace the ones you lost.

Never dip into your income or growth reserves or, worst of all, your ready cash reserve for money to play with.

"What the hell, I'll pay it back someday as soon as I win back the wad I lost."

The hell you will. You'll never pay it back and you will only end up depleting your safe money and going into hock up to your eyeballs. This is the pattern that losers establish time and time again. They are consantly hoping to win back what they lost and reestablish their financial integrity, and they never succeed in doing it.

Fear. Greed. Guilt. Fantasy. Somebody *knows.* This is the debilitating cycle that has to be ended for once and for all times in the future. This is the chain of self-destructive events that must finally be broken. And it can be accomplished only by the acceptance of the discipline outlined above.

Ready reserves, Income, Growth, Speculation. Walking-around money, very safe money, safe money, and mad money. Set up the goals, break your money down into categories, and follow the rules religiously.

Don't get your money mixed up and start borrowing from one category to pay off the debt in another—unless you decide to stick it all in the safer columns and leave it there. Once you start dipping into your safe reserves to speculate on the latest

tip straight from your broker's mouth—sixteen times removed
from the original source, most likely—you are finished. You
will have broken your rules, compromised your goals, and
branded yourself a loser.

CHAPTER THIRTEEN

Follow the Fundamentals

NOW YOU HAVE CREATED a financial skeleton, and your next job is to flesh it out with some particulars. The easiest way to do this is by writing down your goals with the dollar figure beside them.

> Ready cash: $5,000
> Income: $_____
> Growth: $_____
> Mad money: $_____

For each goal there are several investment vehicles available to help you achieve it.

Ready cash: $5,000
Investment possibilities include: day-to-day savings account; money-market funds; treasury bills for $10,000 on up.

Income: $_____
Investment possibilities: tax-free bonds; tax-deferred utility stocks; corporate bonds; preferred stocks; unit investment trusts; tax-deferred annuities; U.S. treasury and government-agency bonds; limited partnerships and low-risk tax shelters.

Growth: $_____
Investment possibilities: selected quality common stocks; convertible bonds and convertible preferreds; certain types of limited partnerships; discounted bonds; gold coins; foreign currencies.

Mad money: $_____

Investment possibilities: hot tips from Lenny, Gil & Co.; aggressive and speculative stocks; high-risk shelters; options; commodity futures; short-selling; ad infinitum.

At this point you are ready to make specific selections for yourself. For each goal you will examine the available investment possibilties and attempt to decide which ones are for you.

Ready cash: **$5,000**

Should you leave your money in the bank or put it into a money-market fund? Since your money is safe in either place, the main consideration should be which one will pay you the higher rate of interst. In my own case I switch my ready cash from my savings account into a money-market fund when the money-market rates exceed bank interest. At this writing the funds are paying better than 10 percent on day-to-day money, so most of my ready cash is there. You might leave $2,000 in the bank and put $3,000 into a money-market fund. Some funds require a minimum of $5,000 to get in, so you can put the entire five grand into a fund and then shift $2,000 back to your savings account later on if you feel the need to diversify. In most cases you are not required to leave a minimum amount in the fund. Some funds will also offer you check-writing privileges, so you have what amounts to a high-yield checking account.

Income: $_____

Think taxes, think taxes, think taxes! This criterion is particularly important when you are investing for income. If you are putting $30,000 to $40,000 into income, you can commit the entire sum to one vehicle, tax-free bonds or tax-deferred utility stocks. If the amount exceeds $40,000, you'd best diversify into two or three areas. Stick to quality securities, A-rated or better bonds and utilities with well-covered dividends and a fairly steady record of both dividend increases and tax deferments. The tax-deferred portion of the dividend will probably vary from year to year, so you will want to select those with a fairly reliable history.

If the income portion of your portfolio is going to exceed $50,000, you may want to diversify further into preferred stocks, unit investment trusts, and other income-oriented investments. Also, if you do not need the income from these investments to help pay your bills, you might consider reinvesting it rather than taking it out and putting it in the bank, which will only provide you with more taxable income. Tax-free unit investment trusts and utility stocks, for example, allow you to plow the dividends back into the securities and accumulate additional shares without paying taxes on the income. Tax-deferred annuities work in a similar fashion. By doing this you are benefiting in two ways: your income is tax-free or deferred, and you are also building up your equity.

Growth: $_____

This is the trickiest area of all since we are talking to a great extent about stock selection and, as we have seen in previous chapters, even the so-called experts have achieved pretty dismal records on this account. I will go into this subject in more detail in later chapters, but we can talk about a few basic rules here. You will minimize your risk when picking stocks for growth if you observe the following rules:

1. Stick to quality stocks only. Stay with the household names, the companies which require little if any explanation about what they do. Reserve the stuff you never heard of, the garbage and "emerging special situations," for your mad money.

2. When investing for growth, *never* buy a stock unless it is yielding at least as much as you can get in the bank, 5 percent or more, and its P/E ratio is under 10. This way, if your timing is wrong and the stock takes two years to really get moving, you will at least get the same rate of return on your money as you would have gotten in the bank while you are waiting for your investment to appreciate.

3. Whenever you buy a stock have a *target in mind*, a price

at which you will *sell a percentage of your position*. It is crucial to lock in profits when they exist since the stock is bound to fluctuate over time. Most people lose money by failing to sell on time. Keep some shares in reserve so you can participate in any further advance the stock makes, but make sure you lock in a profit with part of your holdings. In *The Optimist's Guide to Making Money in the 1980's*, I outlined a plan for buying and selling shares according to various buy and sell signals. The rules do not have to be rigid, but the main criterion is that you take some profits when they exist, and buy additional shares when the price is low again.

4. If the stocks you pick do not move at all after six months or so, consider writing covered call options on them. The better-quality stocks all have listed calls traded on one of the options exchanges. The premiums from the calls will increase your cash flow and, consequently, your annual return.

5. Avoid trading in and out of different issues. Traders wind up losing in the end since it is virtually impossible to keep on picking one winner after another. The percentage will grind you down in the long run. Once you have set up your portfolio of good-quality growth stocks (and this should not be a large number of stocks; three or four issues, never more than five or six no matter how much money you have), stick with it, selling off only a percentage of shares when the prices rise. Only if the stock advances so high that you wind up selling off all your shares of a particular stock should you consider replacing it with another stock. Think of this as a *long-term permanent portfolio*. As long as you continue to like the company, keep holding a position in the stock.

6. Once you have settled on a particular stock, consider buying the convertible preferred or convertible bond, if one is available, instead of the common. The convertible will track the price movement of the common and will provide you with higher income. Convertibles are for both growth and income, a nice combination when you select the right issue.

7. Follow the fundamentals. Fundamental analysis is not

foolproof, but in my estimation it is more reliable than technical analysis or charting. Yes, you will want to know the past price movements of a stock before you buy it. If it has roller-coasted between 25 and 35 for the past two years, certainly you will want to catch it on the lower end of the cycle. This you will do automatically if you observe rule number 2 in this section (high yield, low P/E).

But fundamentals, imperfect as they may be, are the best criteria we have to go with. They supply a dash of reason to an irrational and highly emotional universe. Maybe we should talk about *what's wrong* with fundamental analysis before we go any further.

The main drawback to following the fundamentals is that they are not always reliable. A great deal of guesswork is involved here, no matter how thorough the analyst is, and projected earnings reports are subject to a wide range of variables: a change in economic policy by the government; unanticipated strikes; weather conditions; currency fluctuations; political upheavals in countries we trade with; etc. Analysts have a difficult time forecasting the direction of interest rates, which are dependent on the government's monetary and fiscal policies, and unexpected swings in these rates can play havoc with the fundamentals and, consequently, with the health of the stock market. Major economic developments such as recessions or mild depressions are hard to foresee as little as six months beforehand. Leading indicators are prone to revisions after they are published, and their record for prognostication is not infallible in any event. In December of 1978, half the economists and analysts in the country were predicting a recession for the first half of 1979 while the other half were telling us things were getting better.

Even when the fundamentals hold up and earnings come in as expected, there is no guarantee that the investing public will react accordingly. Many a good stock will just sit there throwing off 7 percent a year and trading at four times earnings while another one is roaring ahead with a yield of less than 2 percent and a market price twenty-five times earnings projected three years into the future. Fundamentals are cold and rational and the public is fickle and emotional. The effort to impose logic on a market which is a reflection of mass psychology, a barometer of the fears and hopes of the multitudes, is often an exercise in wishful thinking more than anything else.

For this reason a lot of people refuse to consider analysis, fundamental or technical, when making market decisions. The random walkers believe that the stock market is nothing more than a crapshoot, and any stocks picked at random have as good a chance of performing well as others selected after careful scrutiny. The Efficient Market Hypothesis maintains that fundamentals are sufficiently analyzed by enough investors so that the news is already reflected in the prices of stocks. In other words, the market tends to discount the fundamentals before they become public.

What all this boils down to is that *no system works perfectly all the time,* so you might as well take a quick look at the fundamentals before you buy a stock since they are the only thing of substance you have to go on. *If* the fundamentals sound good; *if* the company is definitely good-quality; *if* the yield is 6 percent or better and the P/E ratio under 10; *if* you are convinced the company is not going to go belly up any time in the foreseeable future; *if* you are catching it near the low end of its trading range for the past two years or so—then go ahead and buy it. Strikes will come and go, foreign governments will rise and fall, hurricanes and earthquakes will continue to ravage the land, politicians will continue to do stupid and unpredictable things in the stately halls of Congress and the White House, and there is precious little any of us can do about it. If your company is a good one it will survive all the vagaries of nature and all the abuses of man, and its fortunes will continue to fluctuate in the future as they have done for decades past.

So go ahead and buy the common stock or, perhaps, the convertible, collect your dividends or interest as the case may be, write some covered calls when the situation requires it, sell a few shares here and there when the price goes up and buy them back when the price is low again, and you'll find that you will do a lot better over the long run than 95 percent of the people who dump their money into the stock market along with everyone else and chase one lunatic craze after another. If you follow the strategy outlined in this section, you should be able to generate a return of 15 to 25 percent a year on balance over the long haul. That means doubling your money every five years or so, and that means *growth* with a capital G.

Other ways of achieving growth besides buying common stock or convertible securities include shopping around for discounted bonds, that is, those selling under par with a maturity about ten years ahead. This way you will generate a decent income from the interest each year, and you will also have a *built-in* capital gain since the bonds will pay back face value upon maturity.

You might also consider hedging a bit of your money in the gold market. My favorite way to own gold is to buy Krugerrands when gold is under $175 an ounce, and sell them when gold pushes up over $250. If the metal should soar beyond $350 with any conviction by the time this book is published, I might consider raising my buy signal to around $200 an ounce. Other one-ounce bullion coins are also available now if you have an objection to Krugerrands.

Mad money: $_____
This is your play money, your go-to-hell-with-yourself, screw-it-all, have-a-good-time money. Most of us need a little action once in a while. We need to take a chance on hitting the jackpot, on striking it rich; we need to feel we have a shot at turning a modest amount into a million so we can retire in style at an early age. Everyone who works at a job he doesn't particularly enjoy has to have a way of liberating himself from the daily grind. Without this dream most of us could not endure the routine pressures of everyday life. Just keep in mind that the sum you have entered into the space above is your grubstake

money for this enterprise. Don't borrow from the other goal categories if you shoot the works and blow it. Wait until you have accumulated additional funds before trying again.

In Part One we talked about all the ways people lose their life savings. They chase the latest fad stocks, such as the gambling issues during 1978. They get tips from their friends, lovers, and brokers and dive in headfirst expecting to make a fortune overnight. The tips and so-called inside information will always be available, and there is certainly no shortage of brokers around eager to peddle the latest "hot issue" or "special situation" they happen to be working on.

However, if you want to try speculating SMART for a change, use the following techniques and see how you make out.

1. When gold is off in the stratosphere and ASA Ltd., a closed-end trust invested exclusively in gold-mining shares, is selling above $30 a share, you might get an itch to short the stock. Not a bad idea, but the next time the situation arises, instead of shorting the stock buy puts on it. Go out about five or six months and buy puts at a strike price lower than the current market value of the stock. If your timing is right and the bottom falls out of gold, the stock should go to hell, plummet like a Mexican cliff diver, and your puts will increase rapidly in value. You've got a shot at doubling or tripling your money, maybe even better, in a short period of time. Understand that the odds are still stacked against you, as they always are whenever you speculate, but at least you are gambling smart. You are not acting on some hustler's tip, but rather speculating that past fluctuations in the gold market will occur again. You've got a bit of history on your side. Timing is crucial; if you are off by a month or two your puts will expire worthless. But if your timing is right you can multiply your money in extremely short order.

2. Conversely, if the market has been languishing in the doldrums for an extended period, certain bellwether stocks will be flopping around sluggishly at the low end of their trading cycles. Two of the most reliable bellwether companies in recent

years have been IBM and Merrill Lynch, whose fortunes, naturally enough, are tied directly to the stock market. When the market is low and Merrill is selling around $16 or $17 a share, you might try buying calls on it with a strike price of 20 expiring four or five months out. IBM calls should likewise be a good buy at the same time. Again, your timing has to be just right and the market has to start moving up before your options expire for you to make any money. Realize also that when you buy puts and calls you risk losing your entire investment. When you buy a stock at 8 and it drops to 4, you still own a $4 stock. You've taken a beating but you have something left. When you buy options, however, you must be prepared to lose everything if your timing is off.

3. If you want to get more leverage on your money buy on margin, but be sure to confine your margin purchases to your mad-money pool. Always pay in full for your growth and income investments. When you buy on margin you have a chance to get a greater percentage return on your capital. For example, you can buy $10,000 worth of stock for $5,000. If the value of the stock increases to $15,000, you've earned $5,000 on a $5,000 investment and doubled your money. Had you paid in full your return would have been only 50 percent. Remember, of course, that if the stock turns down against you, your equity will drop and you may be subject to margin calls. Your stock will be sold at lower and lower prices to meet the calls and your entire position can be obliterated.

4. If you must act on a "hot tip," adopt the opposite strategy from the one I recommend in the growth section. With good-quality growth stocks I suggested *buying additional* shares when the price dropped. The theory here is that a good company will fluctuate in value over time, and you have a chance to buy more shares at lower prices before the stock advances again.

With speculative issues, however, you cannot take fluctuation for granted. Junk stocks tend to stay depressed once they have fallen. So, if someone advises you to buy Amalgamated Junk at 10 because it is a takeover candidate and will go to 20 in a fortnight, and the stock drops to 8 instead, it's time to get out of the damned thing before it collapses altogether. Set a *loss limit* at 20 to 25 percent below cost on your risk stocks so that you don't get clobbered completely.

Try to have fun with your mad money. You might as well enjoy yourself while you're trying to break the bank. Be prepared to lose without crying. The odds are against you but maybe—just maybe—you'll get lucky one day and hit the jackpot. Have fun, keep a sense of perspective on what you are doing, and don't put up any more money at risk than you can afford to lose.

CHAPTER FOURTEEN

Hire a Broker

YOU ARE FINALLY READY to visit the nearest office of BBF&T and talk to a broker. Should you draw a shark or barracuda as the broker of the day, you are prepared to deal with him on your terms. You have done your homework, learned the jargon, established your financial goals, set up your investment skeleton, and fleshed it out with a few details.

When you sit down at Dale Meredith Worthington's desk and he asks you what he can do for you, you are not going to answer like a loser by telling him you want to "make some money in the market." Not anymore. As a certified member of Investors Anonymous you tell him exactly what you want for your money.

"I want to put $5,000 into your money-market fund. I'm also looking for $20,000 worth of tax-free bonds, A-rated or better, maturing no more than twelve years out and selling at a discount. I want to put another $10,000 into utility stocks with a good record of tax-deferred dividends. In addition, I'm looking for $15,000 worth of good-quality growth stocks yielding at least 6 percent and selling under ten times earnings. And I'd like to take a look at some speculative over-the-counter situations. I've got about $5,000 to put at risk. I'd like you to work up a sample portfolio and get back to me as soon as you can. If I like what I see I'm prepared to do business with you."

The above spiel covers a lot of territory for a sample $55,000 portfolio. But whatever the amount is, $5,000 or more than $100,000, the principle is the same. You are setting the parameters. Follow this procedure with at least two other brokers. In other words, get them competing against each other for your account. Most brokers will be willing to do a little legwork for any amount over $10,000. If you have less than $5,000 to work with, you'd best make your own selections and tell a broker exactly what you want. Only a novice will knock himself out for a small account. You could fib a bit by telling a prospective broker that this is only for starters; you've got more funds coming due in a couple of months that you will be investing in the market. But this is dirty pool. It is better to start off cleanly and honestly if you expect to establish a successful business relationship.

Within a week or two you should have heard by mail or phone from the brokers you approached. If a broker takes longer than this to get back to you, scratch him off your list. He's obviously not that interested in your account for one reason or another. Perhaps he has too many losers on his books providing him with a decent living and he is not interested in dealing with winners.

When you receive the suggested portfolios from each broker, examine them carefully to see if they meet the criteria you've outlined. You should be able to determine after a quick perusal whether a broker spent any time on the project, or whether he dashed it off in a hurry hoping to land a quick account. Once you have decided that a broker's recommendations sound reasonable and are in line with your goals, it is time to make an appointment to discuss your specific purchases.

Here are a few guidelines to follow as you take the next step.

1. *Do not* be intimidated by a broker's arrogance, or an attitude which implies that he knows more than you do about the market so maybe you should just sit back and let him make the selections for you. He may have been in the business for a number of years, but he can't guarantee you that a stock will go up any more than your aunt Nora can. Professionals make mistakes every working day of their lives. If you have done your

homework, you know as much as anyone else which way the market is heading.

2. *Do not* allow yourself to be dissuaded from your original goals if you are convinced they are the right ones for you. Be especially indignant if someone tries to talk you into adopting a more aggressive strategy than you have established. If you take on more risk than you are prepared for, you are the one who has to face the consequences, not your broker, whose money may be tucked safely away in treasury bills.

3. *Do* listen to suggestions that seem reasonable. There may be a legitimate reason why a broker is suggesting a tax-deferred annuity instead of tax-free bonds, or why he thinks corporate bonds are better for you now than utility stocks. As long as the vehicle seems right for the goal in question, there is room for discussion.

The subject of commissions is always a tricky business. Should you or should you not go to a discount house? Should you or should you not ask a broker with a major firm like BBF&T for a discount from the firm's published rates? Again, here are a few basic suggestions.

1. If you are going to make all your own selections and will not be requiring research material or any other kind of service, by all means ask your broker for a 20 percent discount or make your purchases through a discount firm and have your securities shipped out to you. Who knows whether or not the discount house will be in business a year down the road, and even though your securities are fully insured, you don't need any unforeseen complications.

2. If you are going to pick your broker's brain from time to time, if you are going to have him send you research literature and draw up sample portfolios, then he is earning his commissions. He is more than just an order-taker executing transactions at your command.

Still, it is worth broaching the subject of a discount if your account is a substantial one, upwards of $50,000 or so, and/or you will be generating $1,000 a year or more in commissions. A reasonable broker will most likely be willing to give you up to 15 percent off his firm's rates if you are going to be at least a relatively active client. The main thing is that you find someone who is supplying what you ask of him and whom you think you can work with. The rest should follow naturally.

CHAPTER FIFTEEN

Control the Action

THE LEMMING INSTINCT is the major pitfall you should be aware of when committing your money to the market. It is difficult not to get caught up in the euphoria of the moment when everyone else is buying stocks and driving prices up dramatically every day. The opposite is equally true: pessimism is even more contagious than optimism. When the institutions and the masses are dumping stocks by the bushel, depressing the market further from day to day, it takes a hardy soul to resist the panic and avoid the urge to convert dollars into gold ingots, Swiss francs, dehydrated food, and ammunition.

But resist you must if you are going to come out a winner in the end. If financial history teaches us anything it is that most investors do what everyone else is doing according to the prevailing psychology of the moment, and most people lose money in the market. Losers play follow-the-leader from one market cycle into another. The herding instinct is devastating. For some inscrutable reason investors insist on tossing good money after bad, following one another into the market near the tops and stumbling toward the exits en masse near market bottoms. Those who keep their own counsel, acting as individuals and refusing to join the dance of the blind leading the blind, represent an extremely small minority. Most winners are contrarians and they have learned to use mass psychology to their own advantage.

The best buying opportunities do not present themselves that often, and it helps to recognize them when they exist. Perhaps the best gauge of whether you should buy or sell is your broker. When business is good your broker will not have that much time to spend on the phone with you—none at all if you are not calling to place an order. When business is terrible he might be willing to stay on the phone all day; his phone hasn't rung for a week and he is happy to have someone to chitchat with besides his wife and/or girl friend. Try as they may, brokers have a difficult time convincing anyone to buy stocks in a sluggish market. Most people will accept the logic that stock prices are low and this is the best time to buy, before they go up again, but the prevailing pessimism leads them to believe that civilization is finally coming to an end. Conversely, no one has to be talked into buying stocks when the market is booming. Everyone wants to get in on the action and brokers' phones are ringing off the hook with requests for recommendations.

When you call Lenny or Dale, ask him how business is. If he tells you it's been lousy for the past three months, this is probably a signal that the market is about to turn up again. It's time to buy. If he tells you business is just splendid, couldn't be better, and he is willing to hang on the phone discussing the latest flap over Billy Carter, chances are he is lying. Most brokers don't like to admit that they are not making any money, believing reasonably enough that failure breeds failure and success leads to more success. So if Lenny, Gil, et al. have been friendlier than usual lately, this could mean it is time to buy.

An easier signal to recognize is the Dow Jones Industrial Average. Chances are there will be many good buying opportunities available when the DJIA is under 800, and precious few when it is galloping up the mountain beyond the 950 range. You might want to use these figures as a general barometer, remembering that absolute bottoms and absolute tops in any cycle are virtually impossible to catch. We may eventually see the market pushing past 1100 on the way toward heights previously uncharted, never to drop below 1000 again, but I prefer to use past performance as my guide for the time being. Buy below 800 and start taking profits on the way up is a rule which should serve you well in the foreseeable future.

By controlling the action, you will automatically be riding the cycles according to a predetermined plan which is guaranteed to make money for you over the long run. You will be locking in profits as they occur, converting your portfolio into cash as the market continues in an upswing. When the market dips you will be directing cash back into high-yielding securities which have fallen in price. You will be acting independently of the herd, counter to the mass reflex actions of both the institutions and the general public. Your investment decisions will be triggered by various buy and sell signals which you have established in the first place.

The key point here is that *you* are controlling your own financial destiny. *You* are buying and selling when you want to; you are not responding to a broker's breathless exhortation during the frenzy of the moment. Not with your safe money anyway. The income portion of your portfolio is going to be a relatively permanent situation. You may add to it from time to time, but in most cases you will not be selling off existing positions once they are established. The growth portion you will control in the fashion just described. And your mad money is for taking a shot on Lenny's tips.

If you succeed in following these rules, you will have broken free of the fear-greed-guilt syndrome. You will no longer be vulnerable to the emotional twitches of mass psychology. You will be keeping your own counsel, hanging on to your own head when everyone else is running around without theirs, exposing their hard-earned money to a jungleworld of phony tips and unsubstantiated hearsay.

In Part Three I will make some specific investment suggestions. Before we discuss them, however, let's talk about a few more rules for Investors Anonymous.

CHAPTER SIXTEEN

Don't Give Your Broker Discretion

WE HAVE SEEN the shark and the barracuda at work, primarily in the personae of Lenny Harris and Gil Clark. But next to Dale Meredith Worthington, the Billy Graham lookalike with the soul of Barabbas whom we met briefly in Part One, Lenny and Gil are mere pikers.

Dale incorporates the main characteristics of both the shark and the barracuda, and he has developed both styles into a devastating art. He might have written the original book from which Lenny and Gil learned their tricks.

Most brokers adopt the roles which best suit their particular personalities: some are naturally nice guys, others gravitate toward one or another style of selling. Dale, however, is unique. He is not intelligent so much as he is cunning and calculating; not ambitious so much as he is single-minded and driven by a need to acquire massive amounts of money; not good-looking so much as he is imposing, almost frightening in his aspect. He is totally devoid of humor.

To call him a workaholic is an anemic understatement. His entire life is all of a piece. When he is not plying his brokerage trade, he is out collecting rents in his slum dwellings in Jersey City. When he is not buying and selling run-down properties, he is slapping backs at the Rotary Club and grooming himself to run for alderman in his trim and affluent suburban village.

It is impossible to imagine Dale Meredith Worthington enjoying a drink or having a good time with his wife in bed. His every move is measured, every word calculated for effect.

Dale is the type of person who evokes a strong response in everyone who meets him: either you cannot stomach him or else you are totally taken in by his stern, moralistic self-confidence—rather a Jim Jones type leading his cult followers to some fetid utopia in the jungle. Those who are overwhelmed by his presence end up trusting him completely; they become his devoted camp followers. And this trust is the foundation upon which his success as a broker is built. His ultimate goal when he acquires a new client is to gain discretion over the client's account. Discretion gives the broker power of attorney to buy and sell securities in an account on his own initiative, without having to consult the client beforehand.

Now, there are a number of reasons why someone will decide to give discretion over his or her money to another person. Perhaps an individual is too busy earning a living to follow what is happening in the market. Or else he will be traveling abroad for an extended period and needs a trusted fiduciary to look after his affairs. Then again, a good friend might introduce him to a financial guru, a genius with an absolutely unbeatable record for managing other people's money. Whatever the reason, my contention here is that none of these reasons is good enough. Over the long haul most gurus turn out to have feet of clay. Money managers and financial geniuses eventually get cocky and overconfident and wind up looking a trifle stupid —but not nearly as stupid as the clients who gave them carte blanche to handle their legal tender.

In Dale's case, he works the religious angle. True-believing fundamentalists come to him for spiritual advice and end up entrusting him with their life savings. Somehow he makes them feel as though they were tithing and storing up brownie points with the Almighty. Most brokers have a couple of clients who give them at least verbal authority to trade their money without checking in with them first. Paul Marano has a hypochondriac who calls in every day for a prescription for his imagined ailments.

"Hi, Paul."

"Hello, Bruce. How are you today?"

"Oh. Not so good, I'm afraid."

"What's the problem?"

"Everything hurts today. My back, my arms, my head. I was up half the night coughing up phlegm."

"Have you been taking your vitamin C?"

"Fifteen hundred milligrams a day and I still feel like shit. Last week I thought my goddamn lungs would fly out with all the coughing."

"How about your diet? Have you been eating any yogurt lately?"

"Don't talk to me about yogurt. I bathe in yogurt every day, vats and vats of it. Nothing's safe anymore. There's preservatives in everything. Natural food is nothing but a fraud."

"The Russians've been experimenting with B_{15} lately. They say it cures everything from common colds to cancer and heart disease."

"B_{15}? I haven't tried that one yet. You think it's any good?"

"Why don't you give it a try? What've you got to lose?"

"B_{15}, hah? Maybe I should get some, what do you think?"

"I don't see how you can go wrong. It's made from apricot pits, I think. I was thinking of trying it myself."

"You think it'll fix up my lungs?"

"Why don't you keep taking your C and E and B complex with iron, and take three B_{15}'s a day along with them. It'll probably make you feel like a new man."

"That sounds like a great idea, Paul. Thanks a lot. I'm writing this down right now. By the way, how're my stocks doing today?"

"I sold 500 Pittston and 500 RCA on the opening and bought you 1,000 U.S. Steel. You're making money and I expect Steel to take off any day now."

"Good man. You know what you're doing. You're the boss. Thanks again, Paul."

"Don't mention it. The main thing is your health. Let me know how the B₁₅ works out."

Lenny Harris and Gil Clark also have a few clients who let them take discretion over their accounts. Lenny places ads in the personal sections of *The Village Voice* and *Screw* magazine for one of his clients and pimps for him in other ways; Gil gets free basketball and hockey tickets at the Garden for a wealthy attorney client of his. In return these gentlemen give them from $20,000 to $50,000 to run for them on a discretionary basis—money which they can easily afford to lose. These are not unusual cases. While most brokers hunger for discretionary accounts, most find that they are far from easy to come by.

Dale, however, is unique. Discretion for him is a point of moral obligation and, as a result, he has acquired scores upon scores of small investors in the $5,000 to $10,000 range who have given him total power of attorney over their assets. While $5,000 is a relatively meager amount, it can generate whopping commissions when actively traded on an ongoing basis, and enough accounts of this nature can provide a broker with an enviable living.

What makes Dale Meredith Worthington particularly despicable in his humorless ruthlessness is the fact that, unlike Lenny, Gil, and Paul, he is not dealing with hotshot gamblers and good-time Charlies who have money and get suckered in over their heads, only to build up a new stake and come back to play the game another day. Dale's people are hardworking, God-fearing citizens who have deified him for one reason or another. Most of them don't know what he is up to and they really can't afford to lose the nickels and dimes they turn over to him for safekeeping. They are the kind of people most brokers with half a heart consider to be off limits—sitting ducks who are just too vulnerable to take advantage of. It's just no fun without the challenge.

While Dale Meredith Worthington is, admittedly, an extreme

example of a broker run amok with discretionary power, it is usually a mistake to give discretion to anyone, and *always* a mistake to give it to a broker.

The reason for this is the *built-in* conflict of interest inherent in the relationship. All brokers *want* to make money for their clients. The bigger the client, the better they hope to do for them since success ensures a continuing lucrative relationship for both parties. But brokers are, first and foremost, commission salesmen. The more trades they put on the books, the more money they make for themselves. If a broker is absolutely convinced that the market will be in a holding pattern for the next six months, the proper strategy would be to set up defensive positions for his clientele and sit on the sidelines until the market showed some signs of perking up a bit. However, six months of inactivity would put a serious damper on the life-style of any broker. Consequently, either he has to convince himself that the market will continue to be volatile despite all evidence to the contrary, or else he must go scouting for *special situations* (takeover stocks, new gambling issues, a gas-and-oil find, whatever) to justify any trading he does. At this point, the client's interests and the broker's interests are *no longer the same*. Brokers with discretion over a client's money will keep trying to make money for the client, but their own need to earn a living has to take priority. In an active market where most issues are advancing, both broker and client are doing fine so there is no problem. In a sluggish or down market, brokers begin to get a little bit desperate and the discretionary client will be the loser in the long run.

The problem is not so pronounced in the case of an investment adviser, money manager, or some other fiduciary who works for a flat fee instead of for commissions. But even here, a money manager has to show a halfway decent track record over time. If the Dow is up 14 percent and the S&P index is up 16 percent for the year, and a professional financial guru can show an increase of only 5 percent, he is not likely to retain the confidence of his clients too much longer. If the dow is *down*

10 percent and he can't produce a return of 5½ to 6 percent, his clients might as well leave their cash in the bank for a guaranteed 5 or 5½ percent in a day-to-day account. So, even in this instance, the professional working on a fee basis is under enormous pressure to produce or else, and the interests of the client sometimes get misplaced.

Clients are not the only ones who get suckered into discretionary arrangements. Brokers sometimes turn out to be the biggest suckers of all. (Most salesmen will tell you that other salesmen are the easiest marks; they start to believe their own hype when they hear it from someone else.)

At BBF&T a while back a young commodities broker ran a hot streak for his clients that lasted well over a year. Bruno Peroni, a Swiss-Italian transplant, couldn't do a thing wrong. He was hotter than a smoking pistol and he impressed everyone who knew him with his uncanny ability to turn modest sums of money into fortunes in the commodities market. As impressed as anyone else were the brokers who worked around him in the same branch office. The word quickly spread that this man was God. He had charts, he had graphs, he had a pipeline to the high and mighty across the earth and he knew beforehand how every little political upheaval and every act of nature would affect the market for soybeans, cocoa, gold, silver, you name it. Bruno was IT. He KNEW. Look no further. God was sitting in a corner office surrounded by ringing telephones and fawning secretaries.

It didn't take long for him to convince twenty-six brokers in his own branch to give him from $5,000 to $25,000 apiece to run on a discretionary basis. Actually, the word *convince* in the preceding sentence is far too strong. They practically begged *him* to take them on, so many lambs leading themselves to the slaughterhouse. These were professional, seasoned brokers who knew better than anyone else that the commissions on commodities make stock commissions look like welfare handouts. While stock commissions usually average about 2 to 3 percent of the trade (the purchase or sale of $50,000 worth of stock will throw off about $1,000 in commission), money put in the commodities market can sometimes generate *dollar-for-dollar* commissions. If anyone ever had a license to steal, rape, and pillage the countryside, it has to be a commodities broker.

So here were twenty-six of BBF&T's most successful salesmen, experienced streetwise hustlers to a man (and one woman), turning over a total of $364,000 to young Bruno, scion of one of the wealthiest Swiss-Italian families on Planet Earth. Not a bad day's pickings.

It would be unfair to Bruno to say that his luck turned sour immediately; it just seemed that way to his fellow BBF&T salesmen. Actually, Bruno's hot streak lasted about another two weeks, and in that time he had nearly doubled the investments of his co-workers. That was when the bubble burst and Bruno's feet turned quickly to playdough. First, the gold market turned against him. Then it was cocoa, followed quickly by soybeans. Suddenly, the young genius who could do no wrong couldn't even tell the time on his own $5,000 Swiss watch. The smoking pistol turned into a $364,000 ice cube. Everyone was going bust—except Bruno, of course, who knew better than to pump his own money, francs, lira, dollars, whatever, into such a silly venture. Bruno's commission figures exploded like Vesuvius even as his clients and fellow brokers lost their lungs in pork bellies. Rumor had it that one or two (or ten or twelve) of Bruno's office buddies were longing to break one of his arms or one of his kneecaps at least. Rumor had it that Bruno was packing a rod, an American Saturday-night special, to the office each day. Just in case.

Bruno retired very young, a master among professional hustlers. He never really needed the money anyway; another couple of hundred grand on top of twenty or twenty-five million doesn't count for much. He wisely returned to Europe with his kneecaps intact before things got too nasty. But his name will long be remembered at BBF&T. Remembered, but not talked about too much these days. Nobody likes to talk too much about an incident which makes him feel silly, professional salesmen and money handlers included.

While Dale and Bruno are extremes, they are nonetheless real and worth keeping in mind the next time you get the urge to give someone discretion over your money. You should be the one who controls the action, as we discussed in Chapter Fifteen, and when you grant discretion your financial fate is being controlled by others.

If you *must* give discretion for whatever reason, be sure to confine it to the *risk portion* of your portfolio. Serious money is too valuable to take these kinds of chances with.

CHAPTER SEVENTEEN

Don't Sleep with Your Broker and Other Miscellaneous Suggestions

WHENEVER A MAN and a woman come in contact, the potential for sex exists no matter what their original intentions are. This much is a biological given. The point I want to make here, however, is that business and sex can rarely be mixed successfully. If there is one virtually foolproof way to destroy a good business relationship it is to hop into bed with the other party. From that moment on the nature of the association is destined to undergo a dramatic change.

The sexual inclination is all the more pronounced in a broker-client relationship because of the nature of the commodity involved: money. Actual dollars are passed along from one party to another, then back and forth again as various transactions take place. Money and sex, as I mentioned briefly a while back, have always shared a symbiotic relationship. The undercurrent is persistently there, the cultural and biological suggestion that something more ought to be gotten for one's money than mere shares of ownership in a corporate entity. Even when the broker and client are both men (woman-to-woman relationships are few and far between, as we learned in Chapter Eight), the broker is frequently made to feel that he is more of a pimp than an investment counselor. When opposite sexes are linked together by money, the chemistry can be explosive—particularly if one of the partners is available.

Seasoned brokers know that the road to the bedroom is a

dead-end street as far as business matters are concerned; indeed, many have traveled it several times, invariably with disastrous consequences. As a result, they have learned to restrict their amorous activities to their nickel-and-dime accounts, the ones they can risk losing without putting a crimp in their income. There are occasional exceptions where an available female investor will manage to snare a successful broker for a husband or, conversely, where a struggling broker will succeed in marrying a rich woman client. But this is the stuff of which fairy tales are made, the rare exception rather than the rule.

One such fairy tale—or horror story, depending on your point of view—began when a twenty-eight-year-old, out-of-work salesman met an attractive young blonde at an East Side Manhattan singles bar one evening. It didn't take him long to discover that the lady was an heiress who had recently come into an inheritance of $2 million. An incorrigible single who had long resisted the siren call of home, hearth, and love, our salesman was suddenly overcome by an all-consuming swoon. In short order he managed to tickle her fancy, turn her head, and get her to murmur the golden words, *I do.* And so they were married but, alas, not happily forever after, as it turned out.

The unemployed salesman immediately concentrated his energies on the management of his wife's finances, every bit as diligently as he had avoided work in the past. To lend credentials to his newfound occupation, he became a broker at Bull, Banks, Forbes & Trotsky, where, he reasoned, he could earn commissions for himself while managing his bride's portfolio. With an actively traded $2 million account, a broker can earn a handsome living without scrounging around for additional clients.

After six months of churning and burning, the novice broker succeeded in reducing the value of his wife's inheritance to a million and a half. At this point she began to realize that she may have married something less than a financial wizard after all. She directed some ominous threats at the management of BBF&T, suggesting that her husband was taking unauthorized discretion over her account which could have litigious consequences. Meanwhile, the devoted husband managed somehow to transfer about half a million dollars in assets from his wife's name into his own. The heiress claimed she never signed any such transfer papers, whereas her husband claimed she did one night, after her fourth martini, and was just too drunk to remember it.

Matters grew uglier as the weeks flew by. The heiress found it necessary to hire an attorney, but before the case could reach a satisfactory conclusion in court, her husband absconded with her (now his) half million and left the employ of BBF&T without giving so much as ten seconds' notice to his boss. He simply walked out on a Thursday afternoon with his check in hand and never returned. Last heard from, he was living rather comfortably somewhere on the coast of Greece. Or perhaps it was Portugal. The best lawyers have found it difficult to trace his exact whereabouts, and his abandoned wife has all but dropped the case.

While this story is not typical of your average broker-client involvement, it does serve to demonstrate that if it is a good business relationship you are looking for you had best keep it on a business level. In other words, establish your goals and stick to them. Don't complicate things by mixing in some emotional variables you might not be able to control later on. If, on the other hand, it really is sex and/or the companionship of the opposite sex you want, then the atmosphere of a brokerage firm is certainly a more convivial place to hang out in than that of a singles bar. Just remember to give only your mad-money business to the sex objects, and reserve your serious, safe-money transactions for brokers who don't turn you on.

Another miscellaneous suggestion you ought to take to heart is *don't* be taken in by "buzz words." Like all salesmen, brokers are constantly looking for a client's "hot button." What is the precise nature of a client's secret hang-up? What are his hidden weaknesses?

Psychologists that they are, good salesmen understand that most products are not sold through the power of pure reason. An emotional appeal must be made which touches a private chord lying deep behind a client's defenses. This is the most effective way of getting through to someone and, ultimately, getting him to part with substantial sums of legal tender. Is consummate greed the driving force in someone's life? Is kinky sex the key to his basic, subterranean passions? A good salesman has the ability to size up his prey in short order and zero in on his weakness. In other words, a successful broker is usually adept at finding a client's hot button and triggering it with the use of buzz words.

A case can be made that many people's investment habits also reflect their sexual aberrations. Conversations between clients and their brokers are often rife with sexual connotations.

"Hi, Lenny. Jack here. If you hear of something really hot let me know, will you?"

"Looking for a fast mover, are you?"

"A stock that'll give me a quick ride. In and out in a hurry. A fast turnover. You know what I mean."

"I'm onto something very sexy right now."

"No kidding! What is it?"

"Pop Shoppes—3½ a share. Looks like a doubler at least."

"That's exactly what I'm looking for. How long do you think?"

"This one should be a quickie. Two or three weeks, maybe a month at the outside."

"You're sure? I don't want to get stuck with a dog. I'm not looking to marry a goddamn stock and live with it forever."

"This one should be a fast mover, I'm telling you. I wouldn't stick you with a dog. Bing, bang, in and out, take your profit and run like a thief."

"That's what I want. A quick ride and then I'm out. Pick me up 1,000 shares."

Maybe Jack is telling us something about his libido and maybe he isn't, but it sure sounds that way to a lot of brokers and the smart ones know how to exploit this weakness in their clients. Find out what their hang-ups are and tease them along. Sell the sizzle, not the steak. Brokers deal with fantasy more often than with financial reality. The pimp, the pusher, and the broker are selling illusion to all the losers of the world.

In this vein, a broker does not call you up to sell you shares of stock; rather, he may be promoting a hot new issue guaranteed to start performing as soon as you buy it. If there is a touch of the compulsive gambler in your makeup, appropriate language can make the action of the market seem more exciting than a Las Vegas crap game. Brokers learn to play to a client's greatest weakness subconsciously; more often than not they aren't even aware of how they are operating. Psychological subterfuge is second nature to most successful salesmen. Just remember, the natural inclination of even the most honest, unassuming broker is to get you to take on *greater risk* with larger pools of money, and your last line of defense is to *preserve* what you've got and watch it grow through cautious management.

Under the best of circumstances, there is a subtle tug-of-war taking place between you and your broker. Conflict of interest is inherent in the relationship. This much can't be helped and it should serve to keep you on your toes, keep your defenses up. It is up to you to resist, to remain faithful to your goals, to stick to the rules of Investors Anonymous and follow our guidelines.

There is nothing mysterious or magical about the stock market. Stocks have a basic intrinsic value. At any given time the price of a particular company's shares may be undervalued, just about right, or too high in relation to the fundamental health of the corporation. If you think of stocks as just another commodity, like television sets or eggs, a lot of the magic will disappear.

If eggs suddenly soared to $2 a dozen, most people would regard them as too expensive and shop around for a suitable, reasonably priced substitute. After a while the decreased demand for eggs would lead to an overabundance, and the price would start to decline. As the price fell to a more suitable level, say $1 to $1.10 a dozen, demand would pick up again, arresting or slowing down the price depreciation, and eventually driving the price up as demand increased. Admittedly, the market for stocks is not quite so orderly or efficient because of all the psychological ingredients we have already discussed, but it is not totally immune from the law of supply and demand. On balance, over the long run, the market is basically efficient even though it is subject to massive emotional gyrations along the way. It is its *short-term unpredictability* that makes it so fascinating for so many speculators.

By observing the rules of Investors Anonymous, you will automatically erect a defensive wall between yourself and these psychological imbalances. You will actually be profiting from them since you will be converting stocks into cash when mass buying is pushing stock prices way beyond their intrinsic worth, and turning cash back into corporate shares when panic selling depresses them to bargain levels.

Discovering the intrinsic worth of a stock is not a cut-and-dry affair, of course. As I mentioned earlier, the fundamentals are subject to change and there is much guesswork involved in any case. But by zeroing in on a few select issues, following them diligently, and observing the rules regarding yields and P/E ratios outlined in Chapter Thirteen, you have an excellent chance of getting good value for your money. You will have the odds working on your side rather than against you.

In Part Three I will make *specific* stock recommendations for long-term capital appreciation, and in Part Four I will set up model portfolios for lazy investors who don't want to be bothered selecting their own securities.

PART THREE

SOME SPECIFIC
RECOMMENDATIONS

GOOD BUYING OPPORTUNITIES are not always available, and it is important to time your stock purchases just so. The market moves in cycles and you will want to buy stocks at the low end of a cycle, just before the market is ready to begin another upswing. There are times when bonds are a better buy than stocks for capital gain, such as during the fourth quarter of 1979, when long-term interest rates had peaked and were about to start falling. When interest rates drop the prices of bonds begin to rise in value (see my earlier book, *Everything the Beginner Needs to Know to Invest Shrewdly*, for an explanation of this phenomenon).

The last best time for acquiring stocks, as I am writing this, occurred during December, 1978, following the heavy sell-off in the fall. These buying opportunities come around every couple of years or so, and it pays to be patient, observing the cycles carefully, instead of plunging in too early. The following pages contain a list of specific stocks, segregated by industry, which I think are good buys at the *prices indicated* for your long-term growth portfolio.

ADVERTISING

Company: J. Walter Thompson
Symbol: JWT
Exchange: NYSE
Current dividend: $1.80
EPS (last 12 months): $4.40
Buying range: 20–25

Company: Doyle Dane Bernbach Int'l.
Symbol: DOYL
Market: OTC
Current dividend: $1.04
EPS: $3.20
Buying range: 11–15

AEROSPACE

Company: Boeing
Symbol: BA
Exchange: NYSE
Dividend: $1.33 ($1.95 with extras in 1978)
EPS: $7.00 (subject to radical fluctuation)
Buying range: 24–29

Company: Northrop
Symbol: NOC
Exchange: NYSE
Dividend: $1.80
EPS: $6.00
Buying range: 22–26

AIR TRANSPORT

Company: Northwest Airlines
Symbol: NWA
Exchange: NYSE
Dividend: $.80
EPS: $3.36
Buying range: 14–17

APPLIANCE AND TV

Company: RCA Corporation
Symbol: RCA
Exchange: NYSE
Dividend: $1.60
EPS: $3.60
Buying range: 22–25

Company: Hoover Co.
Symbol: HOOV
Market: OTC
Dividend: $.92
EPS: $1.95
Buying range: 10–12

Company: Scovill Mfg.
Symbol: SCO
Exchange: NYSE
Dividend: $1.40
EPS: $3.40
Buying range: 17–20

AUTOMOTIVE—CAR

Company: General Motors
Symbol: GM
Exchange: NYSE
Dividend: $6.00 plus extras
EPS: $12.00
Buying range: 54–58

Company: Ford Motor
Symbol: F
Exchange: NYSE
Dividend: $4.00
EPS: $14.00
Buying range: 36–41

AUTOMOTIVE—DIVERSIFIED

Company: Eaton Corp.*
Symbol: ETN
Exchange: NYSE
Dividend: $2.58
EPS: $7.35
Buying range: 32–36

Company: Bendix Corp.
Symbol: BX
Exchange: NYSE
Dividend: $2.56
EPS: $5.74
Buying range: 32–36

Company: TRW, Inc.
Symbol: TRW
Exchange: NYSE
Dividend: $2.00
EPS: $5.40
Buying range: 22–26

Company: Borg-Warner
Symbol: BOR
Exchange: NYSE
Dividend: $2.00
EPS: $6.00
Buying range: 23–27

AUTOMOTIVE—ORIGINAL EQUIPMENT

Company: Sheller-Globe
Symbol: SHG
Exchange: NYSE
Dividend: $.70
EPS: $2.31
Buying range: 9–11

Company: Arvin Industries
Symbol: ARV
Exchange: NYSE
Dividend: $1.00
EPS: $3.35
Buying range: 12–14

AUTOMOTIVE—REPLACEMENT PARTS

Company: Allen Group
Symbol: ALN
Exchange: NYSE
Dividend: $1.00
EPS: $2.60
Buying range: 10–12

AUTOMOTIVE—TIRE

Company: General Tire & Rubber
Symbol: GY
Exchange: NYSE
Dividend: $1.50
EPS: $5.00
Buying range: 20–23

Company: B.F. Goodrich
Symbol: GR
Exchange: NYSE
Dividend: $1.44
EPS: $4.00
Buying range: 17–20

* Pre-split figures; 3 for 2 split scheduled for Oct., 1979.

AUTOMOTIVE—TRUCK

Company: Cummins Engine
Symbol: CUM
Exchange: NYSE
Dividend: $1.80
EPS: $7.50
Buying range: 28–32

Company: Fruehauf Corp.
Symbol: FTR
Exchange: NYSE
Dividend: $2.40
EPS: $6.35
Buying range: 22–26

BANKS—MONEY-CENTERED/INTERNATIONAL

Company: Continental Illinois
Symbol: CIL
Exchange: NYSE
Dividend: $1.60
EPS: $4.50
Buying range: 23–26

Company: J. P. Morgan & Co.
Symbol: JPM
Exchange: NYSE
Dividend: $2.50
EPS: $6.30
Buying range: 38–42

Company: First Chicago Corp.
Symbol: FNB
Exchange: NYSE
Dividend: $1.20
EPS: $3.40
Buying range: 15–18

BANKS—REGIONAL

Company: Mellon National Corp.
Symbol: MNBT
Market: OTC
Dividend: $1.84
EPS: $4.40
Buying range: 21–24

Company: Philadelphia National
Symbol: PHNA
Market: OTC
Dividend: $2.40
EPS: $4.91
Buying range: 24–27

Company: Chemical N.Y.
Symbol: CHL
Exchange: NYSE
Dividend: $3.16
EPS: $7.75
Buying range: 34–37

BEVERAGES—BREWERS

Company: Anheuser-Busch
Symbol: ABUD
Market: OTC
Dividend: $.88
EPS: $2.40
Buying range: 14–17

BEVERAGES—DISTILLERS

Company: Heublein
Symbol: HBL
Exchange: NYSE
Dividend: $1.52
EPS: $2.66
Buying range: 22–25

BEVERAGES—SOFT DRINKS

Company: Royal Crown
Symbol: RCC
Exchange: NYSE
Dividend: $1.04
EPS: $1.50
Buying range: 10–13

Company: Coca-Cola Bottling, N.Y.
Symbol: KNY
Exchange: NYSE
Dividend: $.44
EPS: $.75
Buying range: 5–6

BROADCASTING

Company: American Broadcasting Co.
Symbol: ABC
Exchange: NYSE
Dividend: $1.20
EPS: $4.75
Buying range: 21–24

Company: Metromedia, Inc.
Symbol: MET
Exchange: NYSE
Dividend: $2.80
EPS: $6.80
Buying range: 37–42

Company: CBS, Inc.
Symbol: CBS
Exchange: NYSE
Dividend: $2.60
EPS: $7.10
Buying range: 40–44

BUILDING MATERIALS—DIVERSIFIED

Company: Wickes Corp.
Symbol: WIX
Exchange: NYSE
Dividend: $1.04
EPS: $3.20
Buying range: 10–12

Company: Johns-Manville
Symbol: JM
Exchange: NYSE
Dividend: $1.92
EPS: $5.25
Buying range: 20–24

Company: Armstrong Cork
Symbol: ACK
Exchange: NYSE
Dividend: $1.10
EPS: $2.26
Buying range: 12–14

BUILDING MATERIALS—RETAILERS

No recommendations

CANADIAN FINANCIAL SERVICES

Company: Canadian Imperial Bank
  of Commerce
Symbol: CM
Exchange: Toronto, Montreal,
  Vancouver
Dividend: $1.60
EPS: $4.23
Buying range: 20–23

Company: Toronto-Dominion
  Bank
Symbol: TD
Exchange: Toronto, Montreal,
  Vancouver
Dividend: $1.28
EPS: $2.24
Buying range: 15–17

CANADIAN MINING

Company: Denison Mines Ltd.
Symbol: DENIF
Market: OTC
Dividend: $1.00
EPS: $2.00
Buying range: 10–13

CANADIAN MINING AND EXPLORATION

Company: Preston Mines Ltd.
Symbol: PRS
Exchange: ASE
Dividend: $.90
EPS: $2.75
Buying range: 10–13

CANADIAN OIL COMPANIES—EXPLORATION

Company: Imperial Oil
Symbol: IMO.A
Exchange: ASE
Dividend: $1.00
EPS: $2.30
Buying range: 16–18

CANADIAN OIL COMPANIES—INTEGRATED

Company: Gulf Canada Ltd.
Symbol: GOC
Exchange: ASE
Dividend: $1.40
EPS: $3.91
Buying range: 22–25

CANADIAN TRUST COMPANIES

Company: Canada Trustco Mort-
  gage Co.
Symbol: CT
Exchange: NYSE
Dividend: $1.52
EPS: $4.00
Buying range: 20–22

CATV

No recommendations

CHEMICALS—DIVERSIFIED

Company: Akzona
Symbol: AXO
Exchange: NYSE
Dividend: $.80
EPS: $1.60
Buying range: 10–12

Company: Diamond Shamrock
Symbol: DIA
Exchange: NYSE
Dividend: $1.48
EPS: $3.25
Buying range: 18–21

CHEMICALS—MAJOR

Company: du Pont
Symbol: DD
Exchange: NYSE
Dividend: $2.75
EPS: $5.75
Buying range: 32–35

Company: Union Carbide
Symbol: UK
Exchange: NYSE
Dividend: $3.00
EPS: $5.45
Buying range: 33–37

Company: Allied Chemical
Symbol: ACD
Exchange: NYSE
Dividend: $2.00
EPS: $4.40
Buying range: 27–30

CHEMICALS—SPECIALTY

Company: Vulcan Materials
Symbol: VMC
Exchange: NYSE
Dividend: $1.60
EPS: $4.50
Buying range: 21–24

COAL

Company: Pittston
Symbol: PCO
Exchange: NYSE
Dividend: $1.20
EPS: $1.50 (should improve sub-
    stantially over long term)
Buying range: 16–20

COMMUNICATIONS

Company: American Tel & Tel
Symbol: T
Exchange: NYSE
Dividend: $5.00
EPS: $7.75
Buying range: 56–60

Company: New England Tel & Tel
Symbol: NTT
Exchange: NYSE
Dividend: $3.16
EPS: $4.27
Buying range: 29–32

Company: General Telephone &
  Electronics
Symbol: GTE
Exchange: NYSE
Dividend: $2.72
EPS: $4.40
Buying range: 26–28

CONGLOMERATES

Company: Northwest Industries
Symbol: NWT
Exchange: NYSE
Dividend: $2.05
EPS: $5.00
Buying range: 22–25

Company: Martin Marietta
Symbol: ML
Exchange: NYSE
Dividend: $2.00
EPS: $5.00
Buying range: 22–25

Company: Ogden Corp.
Symbol: OG
Exchange: NYSE
Dividend: $2.00
EPS: $6.00
Buying range: 22–25

CONSTRUCTION CONTRACTORS

Company: Stone & Webster
Symbol: SW
Exchange: NYSE
Dividend: $2.75
EPS: $5.40
Buying range: 37–40

CONTAINERS—GLASS

Company: Anchor Hocking
Symbol: ARH
Exchange: NYSE
Dividend: $1.20
EPS: $3.30
Buying range: 15–17

Company: Owens-Illinois
Symbol: OI
Exchange: NYSE
Dividend: $1.26
EPS: $3.35
Buying range: 17–19

CONTAINERS—METAL

Company: American Can
Symbol: AC
Exchange: NYSE
Dividend: $2.80
EPS: $5.91
Buying range: 32–35

Company: Continental Group
Symbol: CCC
Exchange: NYSE
Dividend: $2.20
EPS: $4.20
Buying range: 23–26

COSMETICS AND TOILETRIES

Company: Avon Products
Symbol: AVP
Exchange: NYSE
Dividend: $2.80
EPS: $3.95
Buying range: 38–43

Company: Gillette
Symbol: GS
Exchange: NYSE
Dividend: $1.72
EPS: $3.10
Buying range: 21–24

DRUGS

Company: American Home
  Products
Symbol: AHP
Exchange: NYSE
Dividend: $1.50
EPS: $2.20
Buying range: 21–23

Company: Squibb Corp.
Symbol: SQB
Exchange: NYSE
Dividend: $1.08
EPS: $2.60
Buying range: 16–19

ELECTRICAL EQUIPMENT

Company: Gould
Symbol: GLD
Exchange: NYSE
Dividend: $1.72
EPS: $4.15
Buying range: 22–25

Company: Kuhlman Corp.
Symbol: KUH
Exchange: NYSE
Dividend: $1.30
EPS: $2.59
Buying range: 11–13

ELECTRICAL EQUIPMENT—MAJOR DIVERSIFIED

Company: Westinghouse Electric
Symbol: WX
Exchange: NYSE
Dividend: $.97
EPS: $3.55
Buying range: 16–18

Company: General Electric
Symbol: GE
Exchange: NYSE
Dividend: $2.80
EPS: $5.35
Buying range: 40–43

ELECTRONICS—INSTRUMENTATION

Company: Perkin-Elmer
Symbol: PKN
Exchange: NYSE
Dividend: $.52 (low yield, but
   good chance for dividend in-
   crease)
EPS: $2.01
Buying range: 16–18

ELECTRONICS—SEMICONDUCTOR/COMPONENTS

Company: Avnet
Symbol: AVT
Exchange: NYSE
Dividend: $.80
EPS: $2.60
Buying range: 13–15

Company: Texas Instruments
Symbol: TXN
Exchange: NYSE
Dividend: $2.00
EPS: $6.10
Buying range: 55–60

ENTERTAINMENT

No recommendations

FERTILIZERS

Company: Williams Cos.
Symbol: WMB
Exchange: NYSE
Dividend: $1.00
EPS: $1.88
Buying range: 14–16

FINANCE

Company: Beneficial Corp.
Symbol: BNL
Exchange: NYSE
Dividend: $2.00
EPS: $4.20
Buying range: 18–21

Company: Household Finance
Symbol: HFC
Exchange: NYSE
Dividend: $1.45
EPS: $3.50
Buying range: 16–18

FOODS—BAKERS

Company: Campbell Taggart
Symbol: CTI
Exchange: NYSE
Dividend: $1.08
EPS: $2.70
Buying range: 19–21

FOODS—CANNED

Company: H. J. Heinz
Symbol: HNZ
Exchange: NYSE
Dividend: $2.00
EPS: $4.25
Buying range: 30–33

Company: Campbell Soup
Symbol: CPB
Exchange: NYSE
Dividend: $1.76
EPS: $3.69
Buying range: 28–30

FOODS—COMMODITIES

Company: Alexander & Baldwin
Symbol: ALEX
Market: OTC
Dividend: $1.20
EPS: $2.25
Buying range: 12–14

Company: A. E. Staley
Symbol: STA
Exchange: NYSE
Dividend: $1.00
EPS: $1.35 (long-term projection,
　$2.50 plus)
Buying range: 16–18

FOODS—CONFECTIONERY

Company: Russell Stover Candies
Symbol: RUSS
Market: OTC
Dividend: $.80
EPS: $1.67
Buying range: 11–13

FOODS—DAIRY PRODUCTS

Company: Borden, Inc.
Symbol: BN
Exchange: NYSE
Dividend: $1.82
EPS: $4.30
Buying range: 23–26

Company: Kraft, Inc.
Symbol: KRA
Exchange: NYSE
Dividend: $3.00
EPS: $6.40
Buying range: 38–41

FOODS—MEAT PACKING

Company: Esmark
Symbol: ESM
Exchange: NYSE
Dividend: $1.84
EPS: $4.00
Buying range: 22–25

Company: Oscar Mayer & Co.
Symbol: OMC
Exchange: NYSE
Dividend: $1.00
EPS: $1.90
Buying range: 17–19

FOODS—PROCESSED

Company: Kellogg Co.
Symbol: K
Exchange: NYSE
Dividend: $1.32
EPS: $1.90
Buying range: 16–18

Company: Standard Brands
Symbol: SB
Exchange: NYSE
Dividend: $1.48
EPS: $2.70
Buying range: 20–22

Company: General Foods
Symbol: GF
Exchange: NYSE
Dividend: $2.00
EPS: $3.94
Buying range: 26–29

FOREIGN—EUROPEAN

Company: Rank Organ.
Symbol: RANKY
Market: OTC
Dividend: $1.83
EPS: $.70
Buying range: 2½–3

FOREIGN—JAPANESE

No recommendations

FOREIGN—SOUTH AFRICAN

Company: ASA Ltd.
Symbol: ASA
Exchange: NYSE
Dividend: $1.40
NAV: $22
Buying range: 16–18

FOREST PRODUCTS

Company: Georgia-Pacific
Symbol: GP
Exchange: NYSE
Dividend: $1.10
EPS: $2.90
Buying range: 20–22

Company: Weyerhaeuser Co.
Symbol: WY
Exchange: NYSE
Dividend: $1.00
EPS: $2.80
Buying range: 19–21

HOME BUILDERS

No recommendations

HOME FURNISHINGS

Company: Ethan Allen, Cl A
Symbol: ETHNA
Market: OTC
Dividend: $.80 (excellent chance
   for dividend increase)
EPS: $4.28
Buying range: 14–16

HOSPITAL MANAGEMENT

No recommendations

HOSPITAL SUPPLIES

Company: Abbott Laboratories
Symbol: ABT
Exchange: NYSE
Dividend: $1.00
EPS: $2.47
Buying range: 18–20

Company: Angelica Corp.
Symbol: AGL
Exchange: NYSE
Dividend: $.34
EPS: $.92
Buying range: 4½–5½

HOUSEHOLD PRODUCTS

Company: Clorox Co.
Symbol: CLX
Exchange: NYSE
Dividend: $.76
EPS: $1.53
Buying range: 8–10

Company: Colgate-Palmolive
Symbol: CL
Exchange: NYSE
Dividend: $1.08
EPS: $2.15
Buying range: 15–17

HOUSEWARES

Company: Lenox
Symbol: LNX
Exchange: NYSE
Dividend: $1.30
EPS: $3.40
Buying range: 21–24

Company: Mirro Corp.
Symbol: MIR
Exchange: NYSE
Dividend: $.96
EPS: $1.39
Buying range: 9–10

INSURANCE—CASUALTY

Company: Chubb Corp.
Symbol: CHUB
Market: OTC
Dividend: $2.20
EPS: $6.95
Buying range: 29–31

Company: U.S. Fidelity & Guaranty
Symbol: FG
Exchange: NYSE
Dividend: $2.40
EPS: $6.75
Buying range: 24–26

Company: Crum & Forster
Symbol: CMF
Exchange: NYSE
Dividend: $2.52
EPS: $8.66
Buying range: 26–30

INSURANCE—MULTILINE

Company: Aetna Life & Casualty
Symbol: AET
Exchange: NYSE
Dividend: $1.80
EPS: $7.00
Buying range: 25–28

INSURANCE—SPECIALTY

Company: American Express
Symbol: AXP
Exchange: NYSE
Dividend: $1.80
EPS: $4.20
Buying range: 27–30

LEISURE TIME

Company: Brunswick Corp.
Symbol: BC
Exchange: NYSE
Dividend: $.80
EPS: $2.40
Buying range: 10–12

Company: Outboard Marine
Symbol: OM
Exchange: NYSE
Dividend: $1.40
EPS: $3.14
Buying range: 14–15

LODGING

Company: Holiday Inns
Symbol: HIA
Exchange: NYSE
Dividend: $.66
EPS: $2.15
Buying range: 12–14

Company: Hilton Hotels
Symbol: HLT
Exchange: NYSE
Dividend: $1.00
EPS: $2.60
Buying range: 18–20

MACHINERY—AGRICULTURAL

Company: Deere & Co.
Symbol: DE
Exchange: NYSE
Dividend: $1.60
EPS: $4.45
Buying range: 22–25

Company: Allis-Chalmers
Symbol: AH
Exchange: NYSE
Dividend: $1.80
EPS: $6.00
Buying range: 24–27

Company: International Harvester
Symbol: HR
Exchange: NYSE
Dividend: $2.50
EPS: $6.50
Buying range: 26–30

MACHINERY—CONSTRUCTION AND MATERIAL HANDLING

Company: American Hoist &
    Derrick
Symbol: AHO
Exchange: NYSE
Dividend: $1.00
EPS: $2.35
Buying range: 12–15

Company: Clark Equipment
Symbol: CKL
Exchange: NYSE
Dividend: $2.20
EPS: $6.00
Buying range: 28–32

MACHINERY—INDUSTRIAL

Company: Cooper Industries
Symbol: CBE
Exchange: NYSE
Dividend: $1.84 (good chance of
    dividend increase)
EPS: $5.85
Buying range: 36–39

Company: Ingersoll-Rand
Symbol: IR
Exchange: NYSE
Dividend: $3.16
EPS: $6.70
Buying range: 45–49

Company: Joy Manufacturing
Symbol: JOY
Exchange: NYSE
Dividend: $1.72
EPS: $3.16
Buying range: 25–28

MACHINERY—SPECIALTY

Company: Black & Decker Mfg.
Symbol: BDK
Exchange: NYSE
Dividends: $.68
EPS: $1.58
Buying range: 13–15

Company: Ex-Cell-O Corp.
Symbol: XLO
Exchange: NYSE
Dividend: $1.90
EPS: $4.10
Buying range: 21–23

MEDICAL SPECIALTY

Company: Sybron Corp.
Symbol: SYB
Exchange: NYSE
Dividend: $1.08
EPS: $2.50
Buying range: 13–15

MERCHANDISING—DEPARTMENT

Company: Allied Stores
Symbol: ALS
Exchange: NYSE
Dividend: $1.60
EPS: $4.15
Buying range: 18–20

Company: Marshall Field
Symbol: MF
Exchange: NYSE
Dividend: $1.24
EPS: $1.90
Buying range: 15–17

MERCHANDISING—DRUG

Company: Walgreen Co.
Symbol: WAG
Exchange: NYSE
Dividend: $1.40
EPS: $3.61
Buying range: 16–18

MERCHANDISING—FOOD

Company: Safeway Stores
Symbol: SA
Exchange: NYSE
Dividend: $2.60
EPS: $5.25
Buying range: 34–37

Company: Wetterau
Symbol: WETT
Market: OTC
Dividend: $.70
EPS: $1.64
Buying range: 9–10

MERCHANDISING—MASS

Company: J. C. Penney
Symbol: JCP
Exchange: NYSE
Dividend: $1.76
EPS: $4.50
Buying range: 26–29

Company: Sears, Roebuck & Co.
Symbol: S
Exchange: NYSE
Dividend: $1.28
EPS: $2.75
Buying range: 18–20

MERCHANDISING—SPECIALTY

Company: Lane Bryant
Symbol: LNY
Exchange: NYSE
Dividend: $1.00
EPS: $2.18
Buying range: 11–13

Company: Zale Corp.
Symbol: ZAL
Exchange: NYSE
Dividend: $1.08
EPS: $2.52
Buying range: 12–14

METALS—ALUMINUM

Company: Alcan Aluminium Ltd.
Symbol: AL
Exchange: NYSE
Dividend: $2.00
EPS: $7.15
Buying range: 22–26

Company: Reynolds Metals
Symbol: RLM
Exchange: NYSE
Dividend: $2.20
EPS: $5.85
Buying range: 24–27

METALS—COPPER

No recommendations

METALS—DIVERSIFIED MINING

Company: Cleveland-Cliffs Iron
Symbol: CLF
Exchange: NYSE
Dividend: $1.50 (including extras)
EPS: $3.35
Buying range: 22–25

Company: Texasgulf
Symbol: TG
Exchange: NYSE
Dividend: $1.20
EPS: $1.30
Buying range: 15–17

Company, AMAX
Symbol: AMX
Exchange: NYSE
Dividend: $1.80
EPS: $5.00
Buying range: 22–25

METALS—MISCELLANEOUS

Company: GK Technologies
Symbol: GK
Exchange: NYSE
Dividend: $1.10
EPS: $2.35
Buying range: 12–14

Company: Crane Co.
Symbol: CR
Exchange: NYSE
Dividend: $1.40
EPS: $3.60
Buying range: 23–26

METALS—SPECIALTY STEEL

Company: Allegheny Ludlum
Symbol: AG
Exchange: NYSE
Dividend: $1.28
EPS: $2.17
Buying range: 13–15

Company: Carpenter Technology
Symbol: CRS
Exchange: NYSE
Dividend: $1.90
EPS: $3.99
Buying range: 18–21

METALS—STEEL

Company: U.S. Steel
Symbol: X
Exchange: NYSE
Dividend: $1.60
EPS: $2.75
Buying range: 21–23

Company: Bethlehem Steel
Symbol: BS
Exchange: NYSE
Dividend: $1.60
EPS: $4.00
Buying range: 18–22

MISCELLANEOUS

Company: PPG Industries
Symbol: PPG
Exchange: NYSE
Dividend: $1.84
EPS: $5.50
Buying range: 22–25

Company: White Consolidated
  Industries
Symbol: WSW
Exchange: NYSE
Dividend: $1.30
EPS: $4.40
Buying range: 17–19

Company: Occidental Petroleum
Symbol: OXY
Exchange: NYSE
Dividend: $1.25
EPS: $3.00 (depressed earnings
  should improve substantially
  long-term)
Buying range: 15–18

MOBILE HOMES

Company: Skyline Corp.
Symbol: SKY
Exchange: NYSE
Dividend: $.48
EPS: $1.39
Buying range: 8–10

Company: Philips Industries
Symbol: PHL
Exchange: NYSE
Dividend: $.28
EPS: $.89
Buying range: 3–4

OFFICE EQUIPMENT—COMPUTER

Company: International Business
  Machines
Symbol: IBM
Exchange: NYSE
Dividend: $3.44
EPS: $6.00
Buying range: 65–70

Company: Sperry Corp.
Symbol: SY
Exchange: NYSE
Dividend: $1.56
EPS: $5.75
Buying range: 29–33

Company: Honeywell
Symbol: HON
Exchange: NYSE
Dividend: $2.60
EPS: $8.00
Buying range: 42–46

OFFICE EQUIPMENT—COPYING

Company: Xerox Corp.
Symbol: XRX
Exchange: NYSE
Dividend: $2.40
EPS: $5.65
Buying range: 40–44

Company: AM International *
Symbol: AIN
Exchange: NYSE

OFFICE EQUIPMENT—MINICOMPUTER

No recommendations for conservative growth. For speculation, buy National Micronetics (NMIC—OTC) between 10 and 12. Should be 20–25 long-term

* Strictly for a speculative move, buy this stock between 13 and 15 if possible. This is the old Addressograph-Multigraph company, which changed its name early in 1979. Under new management, the stock could be 25–30 intermediate-term, and 30 plus long-term. If the stock hasn't moved by the time this book is published, it should be worth buying at the above price for a long-term hold.

OFFICE EQUIPMENT—MISCELLANEOUS

Company: Dennison Mfg.
Symbol: DSN
Exchange: NYSE
Dividend: $1.00
EPS: $2.75
Buying range: 10–12

OFFICE EQUIPMENT—SERVICES AND SOFTWARE

Company: Itel Corp.*
Symbol: I
Exchange: NYSE

OIL AND GAS PRODUCERS

Company: Houston Oil & Mineral
  ($1.69 cumulative convertible
  preferred)
Symbol: HOI Pr A
Exchange: AMEX
Dividend: $1.69
EPS: $2.35 (convertible into .833
  shares of common)
Buying ranges: 17–20

Company: Louisiana Land and
  Exploration
Symbol: LLX
Exchange: NYSE
Dividend: $1.48
EPS: $2.70
Buying range: 19–21

OIL SERVICES—DRILLING

Company: Reading and Bates
Symbol: RB
Exchange: NYSE
Dividend: $1.00
EPS: $3.12
Buying range: 16–19

* If Itel is still selling below 10 by the time this book is published, pick up some shares strictly on *speculation*.

OIL—INTEGRATED DOMESTIC

Company: Atlantic Richfield
Symbol: ARC
Exchange: NYSE
Dividend: $2.80
EPS: $6.40
Buying range: 42–46

Company: Amerada Hess
Symbol: AHC
Exchange: NYSE
Dividend: $1.00 (plus stock
    dividend)
EPS: $3.75
Buying range: 21–24

Company: Conoco, Inc.
Symbol: CLL
Exchange: NYSE
Dividend: $1.70
EPS: $3.70
Buying range: 23–26

Company: Standard Oil of Indiana
Symbol: SN
Exchange: NYSE
Dividend: $3.00
EPS: $7.40
Buying range: 42–46

Company: Shell Oil
Symbol: SUO
Exchange: NYSE
Dividend: $2.00
EPS: $5.50
Buying range: 27–30

OIL—INTEGRATED INTERNATIONAL

Company: Mobil Corp.
Symbol: MOB
Exchange: NYSE
Dividend: $2.40
EPS: $6.50
Buying range: 29–32

Company: Exxon Corp.
Symbol: XON
Exchange: NYSE
Dividend: $4.00
EPS: $6.00
Buying range: 41–45

Company: Gulf Oil
Symbol: GO
Exchange: NYSE
Dividend: $2.05
EPS: $3.80
Buying range: 21–23

Company: Texaco, Inc.
Symbol: TX
Exchange: NYSE
Dividend: $2.16
EPS: $3.00
Buying range: 22–24

OIL SERVICES—PRODUCTS

Company: Philadelphia Suburban
Symbol: PSC
Exchange: NYSE
Dividend: $1.10
EPS: $3.08
Buying range: 16–18

Company: NL Industries
Symbol: NL
Exchange: NYSE
Dividend: $1.20
EPS: $2.40
Buying range: 15–17

Company: J. Ray McDermott
Symbol: MDE
Exchange: NYSE
Dividend: $1.20
EPS: $4.00
Buying range: 16–18

PAPER PRODUCTS

Company: Hammermill Paper
Symbol: HML
Exchange: NYSE
Dividend: $1.40
EPS: $3.15
Buying range: 15–17

Company: Kimberly-Clark
Symbol: KMB
Exchange: NYSE
Dividend: $2.88
EPS: $6.20
Buying range: 36–39

Company: St. Regis Paper
Symbol: SRT
Exchange: NYSE
Dividend: $1.80
EPS: $3.85
Buying range: 24–27

PHOTOGRAPHY

Company: Polaroid
Symbol: PRD
Exchange: NYSE
Dividend: $1.00
EPS: $3.80
Buying range: 22–25

Company: Eastman Kodak
Symbol: EK
Exchange: NYSE
Dividend: $2.90
EPS: $5.25
Buying range: 41–45

POLLUTION CONTROL

Company: Wheelabrator-Frye
Symbol: WFI
Exchange: NYSE
Dividend: $1.20
EPS: $3.60
Buying range: 24–27

Company: Zurn Industries
Symbol: ZRN
Exchange: NYSE
Dividend: $.80
EPS: $2.25
Buying range: 11–13

PRINTING

Company: R. R. Donnelly & Sons
Symbol: DNY
Exchange: NYSE
Dividend: $1.00
EPS: $3.05
Buying range: 19–21

PUBLISHING—BOOKS

Company: Prentice-Hall
Symbol: PTN
Exchange: AMEX
Dividend: $1.36
EPS: $2.56
Buying range: 19–22

Company: McGraw-Hill
Symbol: MHP
Exchange: NYSE
Dividend: $1.28
EPS: $2.44
Buying range: 15–17

Company: Macmillan
Symbol: MLL
Exchange: NYSE
Dividend: $.72
EPS: $1.65
Buying range: 7–9

PUBLISHING—NEWSPAPERS

Company: Times Mirror Co.
Symbol: TMC
Exchange: NYSE
Dividend: $1.20
EPS: $3.60
Buying range: 20–22

Company: Gannett Co.
Symbol: GCI
Exchange: NYSE
Dividend: $1.76
EPS: $3.05
Buying range: 30–34

PUBLISHING—PRINTING MISCELLANEOUS

Company: American Greetings,
  Cl A
Symbol: AGREA
Market: OTC
Dividend: $.48
EPS: $1.58
Buying range: 8–9

Company: Dun and Bradstreet Cos.
Symbol: DNB
Exchange: NYSE
Dividend: $1.76
EPS: $2.50
Buying range: 23–26

RAILROADS

Company: Santa Fe Industries
Symbol: SFF
Exchange: NYSE
Dividend: $2.40
EPS: $5.75
Buying range: 29–32

Company: Union Pacific
Symbol: UNP
Exchange: NYSE
Dividend: $2.30
EPS: $5.25
Buying range: 38–42

RAILROAD EQUIPMENT

Company: GATX Corp.
Symbol: GMT
Exchange: NYSE
Dividend: $2.00
EPS: $3.60
Buying range: 21–23

Company: Pullman
Symbol: PU
Exchange: NYSE
Dividend: $1.60
EPS: $6.00
Buying range: 22–25

REAL ESTATE—EQUITY AND MORTGAGE

Company: Connecticut General
  Mortgage & Realty
Symbol: CGM
Exchange: NYSE
Dividend: $2.00
EPS: $1.24 (equity/share: $20.00)
Buying range: 16–17

Company: Wells Fargo Mortgage
  and Equity Trust
Symbol: WFM
Exchange: NYSE
Dividend: $1.40
EPS: $1.45 (equity/share: $17.50)
Buying range: 9–10

REAL ESTATE—EQUITY TRUST

Company: Hubbard Real Estate
  Inv.
Symbol: HRE
Exchange: NYSE
Dividend: $1.64
EPS: $2.04
Buying range: 15–16

REAL ESTATE—MISCELLANEOUS

Company: Lomas & Nettleton
 Financial
Symbol: LNF
Exchange: NYSE
Dividend: $1.00
EPS: $1.37
Buying range: 8–10

REAL ESTATE—MORTGAGE TRUST

Company: Lomas & Nettleton
 Mortgage Inv.
Symbol: LOM
Exchange: NYSE
Dividend: $1.85
EPS: $2.20
Buying range: 14–15

REAL ESTATE—PRIVATE MORTGAGE INSURANCE

Company: MGIC Investment Corp.
Symbol: MGI
Exchange: NYSE
Dividend: $1.00
EPS: $2.77
Buying range: 13–16

RESTAURANTS

Company: Chart House
Symbol: CHHO
Market: OTC
Dividend: $.90
EPS: $2.65
Buying range: 13–15

SAVINGS AND LOAN

Company: Great Western Financial
Symbol: GWF
Exchange: NYSE
Dividend: $.84
EPS: $4.00
Buying range: 14–16

Company: Equitable Savings and
 Loan Assoc.
Symbol: EQTB
Market: OTC
Dividend: $1.00
EPS: $5.50
Buying range: 18–20

SERVICES

Company: Saga Corp.
Symbol: SGA
Exchange: NYSE
Dividend: $.44
EPS: $1.86
Buying range: 8–9

SHOES

Company: U.S. Shoe
Symbol: USR
Exchange: NYSE
Dividend: $1.48
EPS: $4.13
Buying range: 18–20

TEXTILE—APPAREL

Company: Levi Strauss
Symbol: LVI
Exchange: NYSE
Dividend: $1.80
EPS: $6.35
Buying range: 25–29

Company: Palm Beach
Symbol: PMB
Exchange: NYSE
Dividend: $1.20
EPS: $3.75
Buying range: 12–14

TEXTILE—PRODUCTS

Company: Collins and Aikman
Symbol: CK
Exchange: NYSE
Dividend: $.72
EPS: $1.90
Buying range: 8–9

Company: Burlington Industries
Symbol: BUR
Exchange: NYSE
Dividend: $1.40
EPS: $2.50
Buying range: 15–17

TOBACCO

Company: R. J. Reynolds
  Industries
Symbol: RJR
Exchange: NYSE
Dividend: $3.80
EPS: $9.25
Buying range: 50–53

TOYS

Company: Mattel
Symbol: MAT
Exchange: NYSE
Dividend: $.30
EPS: $1.30
Buying range: 5–6

TRANSPORTATION—MISCELLANEOUS

Company: Transway International
Symbol: TNW
Exchange: NYSE
Dividend: $1.80
EPS: $4.34
Buying range: 19–21

TRUCKERS

Company: Consolidated Freight-
ways
Symbol: CNF
Exchange: NYSE
Dividend: $1.30
EPS: $4.75
Buying range: 20–22

Company: McLean Trucking
Symbol: MLN
Exchange: NYSE
Dividend: $.64
EPS: $2.74
Buying range: 11–13

UTILITIES—ELECTRIC

Electric utilities are bought primarily for income rather than for growth. When selecting utilities for your income portfolio try to time your purchases when interest rates are relatively high. Most of the time utility stocks behave more like bonds and other fixed-income securities than like other common stocks. When interest rates start to decline, utility stocks generally rise in value and vice versa. Concentrate on those with a good history of dividend increases and tax-deferred treatment of the dividends. Some major electric utilities which meet both these criteria are:

American Electric Power
Current yield: 10.3%
Current tax deferment: 73%

Dayton Power & Light
Current yield: 10.5%
Current tax deferment: 46%

San Diego Gas & Electric
Current yield: 10%
Current tax deferment: 100%

N.Y. State Electric & Gas
Current yield: 10.5%
Current tax deferment: 22%

Ohio Edison
Current yield: 11.7%
Current tax deferment: 100%

Cleveland Electric Illuminating
Current yield: 10.4%
Current tax deferment: 47%

Columbus & Southern Ohio
Current yield: 10.2%
Current tax deferment: 100%

Portland General Electric
Current yield: 10%
Current tax deferment: 100%

Long Island Lighting
Current yield: 10.3%
Current tax deferment: 70%

Niagara Mohawk
Current yield: 10.2%
Current tax deferment: 10%

Philadelphia Electric
Current yield: 11%
Current tax deferment: 41%

Pennsylvania Power & Light
Current yield: 10.5%
Current tax deferment: 40%

Public Service Electric & Gas
Current yield: 10.1%
Current tax deferment: 75%

UTILITIES—GAS DISTRIBUTION

Company: Arkansas Louisiana
   Gas Co.
Symbol: ALG
Exchange: NYSE
Dividend: $2.20
EPS: $4.24
Buying range: 28–30

Company: Columbia Gas System
Symbol: CG
Exchange: NYSE
Dividend: $2.44
EPS: $3.94
Buying range: 24–26

Company: Pioneer Corp.*
Symbol: PNA
Exchange: NYSE
Dividend: $1.92
EPS: $3.68
Buying range: 23–25

* Could split 2 for 1 by the time this is published.

UTILITIES—GAS PIPELINE

Company: El Paso Co.
Symbol: ELG
Exchange: NYSE
Dividend: $1.32
EPS: $2.37
Buying range: 13–15

Company: Texas Gas Transmission
Symbol: TXG
Exchange: NYSE
Dividend: $1.46
EPS: $3.00
Buying range: 16–18

Company: Tenneco
Symbol: TGT
Exchange: NYSE
Dividend: $2.20
EPS: $4.53
Buying range: 27–29

Company: Northern Natural Gas
Symbol: NNG
Exchange: NYSE
Dividend: $3.00
EPS: $6.15
Buying range: 32–34

SPECIAL NOTE: Companies frequently split their stocks or offer stock dividends which affect prices. The above figures reflect prices of stocks as they existed in the early fall of 1979. Where splits are pending I have noted them. Readers are cautioned to check appropriate sources for information on splits and stock dividends which will affect the figures published here.

PART FOUR

MODEL PORTFOLIOS FOR THE LAZY INVESTOR

AT THIS POINT in our financial odyssey you are better equipped to make money in the stock market than the great majority of people who have ever invested a nickel. By following the rules of Investors Anonymous, selecting stocks from my list of recommendations, and buying and selling according to my target numbers, you should come out a solid winner over the long run. However, if you feel that you can't be bothered spending the small amount of time required to pick and choose your own portfolio and to track the daily prices in the financial pages of your local newspaper, I will simplify the whole procedure even further for you.

Let's assume, as we did earlier, that you are in a 32 percent or higher tax bracket. You own the house or apartment you live in and your income is sufficient to pay your monthly bills. Here are some sample portfolios you can establish depending on how much cash you have.

$5,000

Leave your money in the bank or call up the nearest branch office of a major brokerage firm and deposit the money in a money-market fund if the current rate of interest is higher than the banks are paying on day-to-day savings.

$10,000

Leave $5,000 in the bank or in a money-market fund.
Buy 300 Sheller-Globe at 11 or less or 300 Hoover Co. at

12 or less. If these prices have risen beyond buying range, try to buy 300 Russell Stover Candies at 13 or less. When you buy the stock, tell your broker to sell 100 shares if the price hits 15, another 100 shares at 18, and the final 100 at 21. Buy the stock back when it falls within buying range again.

You'll have between $1,000 and $1,500 to speculate with. If gold is $300 an ounce or more and ASA is over 30, buy puts at 30 expiring 6 months out. If the DJIA is under 800 and Merrill Lynch is selling for less than $20, buy calls at 20 expiring in 6 months.

$20,000

Leave $5,000 in a bank or a money-market fund.

Buy 300 Sheller-Globe or 300 Hoover if they are in buying range. Also buy 400 GK Technologies for 14 or less or 400 Allegheny Ludlum for 15 or less. Give an order to your broker to sell off 100-share lots as the stocks hit increments of 3 points above your purchase price. Start accumulating the stocks again as they decline within buying range.

Using the parameters outlined a moment ago, put part of your $5,000 mad money into ASA puts or Merrill Lynch calls. Buy 20 Krugerrands or other one-ounce gold coins if gold is under $175 an ounce; sell them off 5 coins at a time as gold pushes back up through $250.

$50,000

Leave $5,000 in a bank or a money-market fund.

Buy 500 American Electric Power, 700 San Diego Gas & Electric, and 500 Long Island Lighting. Total tax-advantaged income investment is approximately $30,000.

$10,000 should go into growth in the manner prescribed immediately above: buy 300 Sheller-Globe or 300 Hoover plus 400 GK Technologies or 400 Allegheny Ludlum. Sell off 100 shares of each on 3-point rising increments, and buy them back when they return to buying range.

Speculate with the remaining $5,000 in the way we already outlined, or commit the entire amount to a managed commodities program. Some of these have established excellent track records on balance over the long run.

$75,000

Leave $5,000 in a bank or a money-market fund.

Buy 500 American Electric Power, 700 San Diego Gas & Electric, and 500 Long Island Lighting. Buy $20,000 worth of general obligations bonds issued by the state you live in. Ask for discounted bonds maturing within ten years. Or, buy 20 units in a short-term, tax-free bond trust. Total tax-advantaged income investment is approximately $50,000.

Fifteen thousand should go into growth. Buy 300 Sheller-Globe or 300 Hoover, 400 GK Technologies or 400 Allegheny Ludlum, and 200 RCA or 200 Northwest Industries or 200 U.S. Steel, all at 25 or less. With any of these last three suggestions, sell 100 shares at 30 and the last 100 shares at 35. Buy them back when they return within buying range.

This leaves you $5,000 to speculate with in any of the ways already mentioned.

$100,000 and over

Leave $5,000 to $10,000 in a bank or a money-market fund.

Buy 500 American Electric Power, 700 San Diego Gas & Electric, 500 Long Island Lighting, and 500 Portland General. Also buy $30,000 worth of tax-free bonds or bond units in the manner described above. Total tax-advantaged income investment is approximately $70,000.

Allocate $20,000 plus to growth. Put the money into three or four stocks, definitely no more than five, buying several hundred shares each of the companies already mentioned. If you can't find any of them within buying range, chances are the overall market is too high and it is not a good time to buy growth stocks. If this is the case, buy more utilities and tax-frees and wait for the market to fall, creating new buying opportunities.

Under no circumstances should you speculate with more than 10 percent of your assets. When playing with $10,000 or more, try three different speculative ploys. Buy $3,000 to $4,000 worth of a high-risk stock, short Merrill Lynch when it is trading above $30 a share, buy calls when it is under $20, buy puts on ASA when it is over 30, buy gold coins when the price of the yellow metal is under $175.

Have fun, control the action, and don't risk more than you are prepared to lose without plunging into deep despair.

POSTSCRIPT

As I AM WRITING this the Dow Jones Industrial Average has just closed at 877, near its high for 1979. Many of the stocks I recommended in Part Three have already moved substantially beyond their buying ranges. Those following the rules of Investors Anonymous would have accumulated stocks in December, 1978, the last best buying opportunity to date, and would now be taking profits with part of their holdings and putting the proceeds into a money-market fund, which is currently yielding over 10 percent.

It is difficult to say where the market will be by the time this book is published, but I do want to caution you against one impulse you may have. DO NOT jump in and buy stocks above their buying ranges if the market is still strong simply because you want to get started on this program. Be patient and wait until the market has fallen again and good buying opportunities are available once more. Good buying times have always come around every few years or so, and there is no reason to believe this will not be the case in the future.

If the DJIA should push ahead strongly into the 1100–1200 area, and hang in there with any conviction, it may eventually be necessary to upgrade my buy signals. This is what happened with gold, which I originally suggested buying under $150 an ounce and now would start accumulating cautiously below $175. But at present I see no reason to start buying stocks above the prices I mentioned in Part Three. Since this is a book and not a weekly market letter, you will have to be your own best judge of whether or not you deem it wise to buy stocks above my suggested price ranges.

If you have any specific questions you would like to direct to me, you can reach me care of my publisher. Your mail will be forwarded and, if you have enclosed a self-addressed stamped envelope, I will answer you as soon as reasonably possible. Any letters addressed to Bull, Banks, Forbes & Trotsky, however, are apt to be returned as undeliverable by the Post Office.

JEROME TUCCILLE

Cos Cob, Connecticut
September, 1979

Date Due

FE15 97			
DEC - 8 1997			
JUN 2 9 2000			
DEC 1 3 2001			